THE JOURNEY OF FAITH

The Journey of Faith

LIELA MARIE FULLER

Jadora's Child Publishing

CONTENTS

Dedication		vii
1	The Middle Passage of Faith	1
2	Jump!	3
3	Learning How to Fly	11
4	One Word from God Can Change Everything	19
5	Fly Liela-Beans Fly	24
6	Stretching Our Wings	35
7	Gaining Strength	39
8	Growing in Faith	41
9	Learning to Balance and Believe	45
10	Flapping Our Wings	51
11	Going Through the Flood	56

12	Moments of Rest	60
13	Hitting the Rocks	63
14	Regaining Flight	66
15	A Moment of New	73
16	Windshears and Freefalls	80
17	Shelter Day: Refusing to Give Up	83
18	Breathing Room	85
19	Taking Flight Again	91
20	Finding Home	95
21	Losing Yet Gaining Everything	104

About The Author	108

DEDICATION

Mommy: I always thought you would be here to read this. You were my forever cheerleader and I miss you immensely. I'm thankful I know you are in Heaven with Jesus, but I miss your presence every single day. I love you more and that's finally, finally it.

~~

Elder Karen: I only wish you were here to read this book because I know you believed in me. I love and miss you! I will always treasure these three words from you, "Love You, Honey." I often tried to tell you how those words made me feel, but I couldn't speak through the tears. But somehow, you understood. For that and so much more, I am forever grateful.

Copyright © 2020 Liela Marie Fuller
ISBN: 0-9961289-1-3
ISBN-13: 978-0-9961289-1-9
Library of Congress Control Number: 2017905366

All rights reserved. No part of this publication may be reproduced, distributed, or transmitted in any form or by any means, including photocopying, recording, or other electronic or mechanical methods, without the prior written permission of the publisher, except in the case of brief quotations embodied in critical reviews and certain other noncommercial uses permitted by copyright law.

Jadora's Child Publishing
PO Box 44762
Eden Prairie, MN 55344
jadoraschild@gmail.com

Ordering Information:
Quantity sales. Special discounts are available on quantity purchases by corporations, associations, and others. For details, contact the publisher at the address above.

Printed in the United States of America
First Printing, 2021

| 1 |

The Middle Passage of Faith

Unlike the middle passage of slavery, the middle passage of faith is a choice. It is a day-to-day and sometimes moment-to-moment decision to walk in faith no matter what you see. The middle passage of faith is that time between stepping out on faith and actually walking into the manifestation of a God-sized promise. Unfortunately, it's something many people gloss over when sharing their stories.

Before taking my leap of faith, I often wondered about the middle. I would often hear men and women of faith discuss how they made it through this trial or that trial with very little detail about the middle of the journey. Their stories always seemed to have a beginning and an end, but very few talked about what happened in between, what I call the middle. I rarely heard them discuss how difficult it was to obey God at any cost. They discussed their yeses and their successes, but they hardly ever discussed whether they had moments of doubt, fear, or frustration.

I have taken several leaps of faith in my lifetime, and few people know how my middle looked and felt. Most people would have no idea of the tears I cried or the insane number of times I wanted to quit. I believe the middle is just as important as the beginning and the end. The middle builds character, cements faith, and encourages trust in God. We cannot get to the end of a journey without a middle passage. We do not just transport from one place to another. I hope as you follow along with me, you will be encouraged that you are not alone when you face trials after trusting God. I'm here to tell you to trust God anyway. Jump!

| 2 |

Jump!

In 2013, my son and I were living a good life in Connecticut. We were living in a home we loved, my son was going to a great school, we were a part of a beautiful church family, and I had a fulfilling career. Life was good. We didn't have everything we wanted, but we absolutely had everything we needed.

But soon things began to shift for me. I did not know what was happening or why, I just knew that things felt different.

In July 2013, after having surgery and recovering at home for six weeks something strange happened. I was preparing to return to work, but I found I had no desire to reenter corporate America. I thought maybe it was the customary dread of returning to work after having significant time off, but even after getting back into a routine, I couldn't shake the feeling that something was amiss but I could not put my finger on it.

It was like someone flipped a switch. I was no longer interested in the job I enjoyed for more than a year. As I look back on it, I can say that there was a lot that led up to that feeling. Before the surgery, things were going well and whatever feelings I had about the job, I suppressed them because the job was my plan. It was what I needed to do until I could officially leave to pursue my dream of becoming a full-time author and entrepreneur. I was already on my way to my goal, with the release of two books and the launch of my first business, but at the time neither was making me enough money to sustain our lifestyle. My goal was for the job at the firm to be my last job.

When I came back to work after having surgery, I was different; I was unhappy with the job, but I knew that I did not want another job. In fact, I was ready for my long-term goal of being self-employed to become my short-term goal. The firm had also changed and while I couldn't put my finger on exactly what was happening, I knew it was something I didn't like. I realized that what I was feeling was a need for something new, something different. I thought that I could shake the feeling somehow. I thought that I would get over it after being back at work for a few weeks, after all, I had rent and a car payment to make so just leaving my job was not an option for me – not without a serious backup plan.

During this time, my relationship with Christ grew tremendously. It got to the point that all I wanted was more of Him. I yearned to spend time in His presence – praying, worshipping, and listening to what He would tell me. I would get up extra early, get myself ready for work, and take the time to pray, read my Word and bask in His glory. The more time I spent with God, the more uncomfortable I got at the prospect of staying at the firm.

I continued writing while waiting for the right time to resign. I wrote and released my second book, *Love Letters of a Worshipper*. The book contained love letters to God inspired by time spent in God's presence. I launched the book and was thrilled to see it hit number one on Amazon's best-seller list for its category. However, my excitement was bittersweet. Even though I had a number one book on Amazon, the funds coming in were not enough for me to leave my job, so I continued to work.

Despite a lack of motivation, I still took my job seriously and I was still good at it. Unfortunately, my skills intimidated my coworkers. Instead of appreciating my wealth of applied knowledge and ability to build relationships with clients, they resented me - and they didn't bother to hide their disapproval. I understood it, but I tried not to allow it space in my thoughts. I just wanted to do my job and pay my bills.

As I grew in faith, I had to repent from the backbiting and gossip that I had participated in on the job. As a part of that repentance, I decided to leave whatever room I was in if backbiting or gossip began. After a while, it became clear to my co-workers that I would not participate in backbiting or gossip anymore, and, I became the target. I was no longer the one that they told their gossip to; I was the one they talked about and that was fine with me;

The next year or so, life at work was difficult. My coworkers continued to denigrate my work and my character. They tried to be discreet, but I was always aware of what was going on. I tried my best to ignore their snickers, but things got worse when the IT Director asked me to lead a multimillion-dollar project.

Ironically enough, no one wanted the project when I started it. It was only after I was successful that my colleagues wanted their names on it. However, management recognized it was me putting in the research after-hours to make this project work. I received the credit, and my coworkers' resentment grew. They wanted me gone, but truthfully, I wanted the same thing.

During the Spring and Summer of 2015, the firm began laying off people from various departments one by one. Each time we received notice of a layoff, I wondered if I would be next. One day as I was driving in, my phone began to go off with text messages from the one coworker who was still a true friend in my department. His text messages were ominous. He said that all of the offices were laying people off, including the one we worked in. He told me it was a blood bath, and he was right. By noon eleven people had lost their jobs, and we all knew that the firm was in trouble. I secretly hoped that I would be one of the people laid off that day, but I was not. There seemed to be a reprieve from my frenemies that day because they were all afraid of losing their jobs. While I had never been laid off before, I was not scared. I thought if they were to let me go, I could collect unemployment and work on my businesses full-time, but that did not happen.

After the initial layoffs, I prayed and sought God's counsel because I still did not want to be at the job, but I knew I couldn't leave. I wanted to go and be self-employed, but I could not see how to do that without Him. God told me that if I prayed sincerely for the firm's success, He would release me from the job. At first, I did not want to do it, but I knew that I trusted God, so I humbled myself and obeyed God. I prayed that the firm's business would pick up and that the atmosphere would change. I interceded for my coworkers who lost jobs. I went to God daily seeking His favor and His will for the company I worked for, and while I was in this season of prayer, the firm seemed to settle, and there were no more layoffs while I was there.

As I continued praying, God began to open miraculous doors for me. One day, I received an email from a major computer corporation requesting my presence at their annual showing of new products in Florida. My first thought was, "This is a scam," and I almost deleted the email. But as I gave it a quick scan, something caught my attention.

The email stated that the host corporation would pay for my hotel and meals, but I received emails like this before, so I was skeptical. The email contained a link to the hotel where this meeting was to take place and since I had never heard of The Diplomat Hotel, I clicked on the link, and all the skepticism I had about the trip vanished. As soon as the site opened, I was transported to sandy beaches, beautiful rooms with ocean views, stunning rooms, and so much more. I could see myself laying in a cabana enjoying the sun while listening to the water hit the shore and at that moment, I knew that I had to go. I registered right away not knowing if the firm would agree to send me or not, but I was going no matter what. After I registered, I sent my manager an email asking if I could use our department's training budget for my flight. I also asked if I could record the days, I would be absent from the office as training days instead of personal vacation time. I tried to be patient as I waited for my manager to get back to me, but I was anxious. I knew there had been a negative shift in our relationship, but I hoped she would still approve of the trip.

Unfortunately, she didn't. Not only did I have to fund my own flight, but I also had to use the last of my vacation days to go to the training. I realize now that the situation was probably more toxic than I knew. I have learned that sometimes God must make things (people, places, and things) uncomfortable for us to have the courage to move on. That's what He was doing for me at the firm.

The same day my manager told me she wouldn't authorize the firm to pay for my flight, a representative from the company hosting the event reached out to me directly to ask if I was still coming. I explained that I could take time off, but my firm was unwilling to pay for my flight. He responded, "Is it just the flight that you need?" I said that it was, and his response almost knocked me out of my chair, "I believe we can take care of the flight for you. Just let me check with my team."

I was outdone! That evening I met with my Bishop regarding Church business, and as we were ending our meeting, he told me to make sure I got some rest. I was floored because I had not mentioned the trip to him, but I felt like his statement to me was complete confirmation that this trip was from the Lord. I explained to my Bishop about the trip and what I needed to be able to go, then I asked him to pray with me regarding the flight. He agreed with me in prayer that the company would pay for my flight, and before I arrived home, I had an email from the company representative stating that the flight and car service to and from the hotel was approved.

I was ecstatic and ready for this time away. I didn't know what was going to happen for me while I was away on this trip, but I was eager to see what was in store for me. I kept looking at the hotel's website envisioning myself walking through the lobby and relaxing by the water. I could almost see myself sitting on one of the warm beaches with sand in between my toes.

I arrived at the airport excited for this amazing getaway. I thought about bringing my son, Malachi, with me, but I would have to pay for the extra plane ticket and that was not an option, so Malachi stayed home.

As I journeyed on the flight to Florida, I was reminded that about a year before this trip, I wrote a prayer to God in my journal asking Him to send me on vacation. I told Him that I was tired, and I asked Him to send me away. I asked Him to provide everything that I needed for the vacation – the food, the way to get there, everything. I wanted to go somewhere and just rest. A year later, here I was going on vacation to a beautiful resort to look at computers on someone else's dime, it was the perfect respite for me.

When I arrived at the airport in Florida, I had no idea where the car would pick me up, so I panicked. I never had a car and driver sent for me, so I did not know they typically waited by baggage claim. I called the service, and they guided the driver to me.

After my driver found me, he took my bags and escorted me to the car – a brand new Mercedes M Class SUV. I have a thing for cars, so I was thrilled. I tried to contain myself so I wouldn't look uncivilized, but this was an amazing start to my vacation. The driver put my bags in the back and opened the passenger door for me. As we drove along the roads to get to the hotel, the driver told me about the area and some of the sites I should look for while I was in the area. He also mentioned an annual car show that I'd just missed. I thought about coming back for a car show the following year. As we approached the hotel, I could see the amazing lights from the top of the hotel and I was excited. The hotel was more beautiful in person than it was on the website. God had not only answered my prayer; He exceeded my wildest expectations.

When I walked into the hotel, I was blown away. There was a line of palm trees in the lobby with large, beautiful windows and doors that opened right up to the ocean. It was like the water was inviting you to come out and enjoy it; even though it was after dark, I could still hear the waves crashing along the shore and I couldn't wait to get outside. The lobby was bustling with people, but it was not loud at all. There were chairs everywhere but there was still plenty of room to walk and get where you needed to go. When I got to my room, it was one word – stunning!

The first thing I saw was the view – from the moment I walked into the room I could see the water and as I walked further into the room, the view just got better. I could see the city and it seemed like there were water views on every side. As I surveyed the room, there was a plush king-size bed, and the bathroom was luxuriously well-appointed. I could not believe this was my room for the next three days. I could not wait to get up in the morning to see the ocean and the intercostal views in the light of day.

As if the room and the flight were not enough, I noticed an in-room coffee maker with Starbucks coffee. I really could not wait to go to sleep and wake up now. Having Starbucks coffee in the room was like a kiss from God Himself. He sent me on vacation just as I asked Him nearly a year before, and He took care of every single detail, including making sure that the room had the kind of coffee I loved to drink. All of this just to remind me just how much God loved me and all I could do was cry.

For three days and two nights, I basked in every blessing God provided: delicious meals, great company, and a fantastic suite. I even walked along the sandy beaches allowing the sand to find its way between my toes. I wanted to hang out in the water, but it was too cold because of the impending tropical storm. Nevertheless, I stood in the sand and breathed new air and I felt rest. I saw God in clouds and while others saw an impending storm, I felt nothing but peace.

When I boarded the flight to leave Florida, I was a different person. God confirmed that He was with me, and He would be with me on the next part of my journey. After obediently praying for a company that had caused me so much strife, God had blessed me with a dream vacation. My faith was elevated. I believed that if God could provide my dream vacation once, He could set up my life such that what I experienced in Florida could be a way of life for me. A couple of days after I arrived back from Florida, I received the Lord's blessing to resign and I did just that.

When I gave my 2-week notice, everyone was stunned because I was not going to another job. I was leaving to be an author and run my businesses full-time. My manager and co-workers all thought I was joking, and most of them operated as if I was not leaving. But I was encouraged by God's blessing. In my mind, God had just sent me on an all-expense-paid vacation, so surely He could send paying clients and customers my way.

On the outside, I was excited, but on the inside, I was terrified. I knew God told me to leave the job, but I had nothing except Him to fall back on. If you've ever been on any faith journey, you know that total reliance on God is the scariest part.

Before leaping into entrepreneurship, I was living paycheck to paycheck, and although I knew I had God's blessing, I had no idea how He was going to come through. I needed a foundation, so I set up meetings with my Bishop and my prayer mentor.

They both provided great strategies for how to get through this new season, but I was still nervous. I was finally doing what I felt called to do, but it would only succeed if I could turn my supplemental income streams into primary resources. In all honesty, I wasn't sure how to get the checks from my books and businesses to sustain me. But I was determined to trust God.

Just a few days before I left my job, the Human Resources Administrator called me to let me know they were sending over my exit package. The administrator wanted to know what I wanted to do with the funds from the savings account the firm had secured for me. I had forgotten all about it! I asked how much money was in the account and was stunned to find out I had accumulated over $8000. Since I had been at the company for more than three years, I was able to take the full amount minus taxes. Unexpectedly and by God's grace, I had more than $6000 to sustain myself and Malachi while I worked on building my businesses.

| 3 |

Learning How to Fly

The first couple of weeks of being self-employed felt a bit like vacation, but I knew I needed to work harder than ever. After all, I was no longer receiving a paycheck so the money that I had to work hard to get book sales and clients to keep a steady stream of income coming into our home. We had my savings, but I knew that would not last forever and I wanted to be sure my business was in a good place before we arrived at that point.

Before I left the job, I established two businesses – a publishing company and a computer support company. I started both because I saw the potential to make money while helping others. When I left the job, I had a list of clients under my computer support company that I thought would provide a stable income. I knew that there needed to be an increase in both businesses, but I believed that business could increase if I put in the work. I was also commissioned to do book trailers, website videos, and other videos for clients. This was something I picked up while volunteering at my church and when people realized it was something I could do well I was able to use that as another stream of income.

Clients began coming into my computer company regularly which was a very good thing. The only bad thing is the typical client was a one and done so I had to find a way to make residual income with these clients, so I decided to offer online classes and instructional videos. The training videos were time-consuming to create and they did not pick up much traction so I focused on what I knew and began to really market the business to bring in new clients.

During this time my worship time with the Lord was producing more books, more instruction, and more wisdom. I worked daily to push out new content on my websites, social media pages, and even in my books and blog. I used the funds I received from the firm to cover our expenses and continued to implement the strategies laid out for me before I left the firm. I felt confident that we would be just fine, I just needed to get a certain amount coming in every month and we would be set. I figured that if I brought in close to what I was making (or even a little less) we could make it easily, but as Christmas approached it seemed like the clients I had started to dwindle and the promises made by those who wanted my services did not come through.

By January, the funds I received when I left the firm were depleted, clients that were supposed to be sure things disappeared and despite my best efforts in the business and book promotions, book sales virtually dried up as well. I was unwilling to give up because I knew that God told me to leave the job. I believed I was on the right track and while things seem to not be going the way I thought, it did not shake my faith in God but I did wonder if I did everything I was supposed to do. I prayed every day and God continually spoke to me, so I believed that if I were not doing what He wanted or needed me to do He would've told me and I knew that because I asked Him frequently. I knew that God had a plan for me and I knew that the plan was great, but I just needed to trust Him fully no matter what.

By January 29th, things had gone from bad to worse and I had to do something I never thought I would have to do again – go to the food bank. When I was a young girl, I would go to the food bank with my great-grandmother or my mother and as I became a teenager I vowed that I would never have to go to a food bank again. But here I was in need and I had no place else to turn. That day, I sat in the food bank needing food, money, and more and all I could do was journal my feelings about it. Writing has always been the way that I process things and this situation was no different:

It's January 29th and my best friend is turning 40. I turned 40 a little over a month ago and today on my bestie's birthday I'm sitting here at the food bank. Today is the official launch and release day for 2 of my books and I'm waiting at the food bank to get food. I'm a published author, CEO of two companies and I'm in need of not just food but services. My electricity is past due, my rent is past due, my cable is off and I still believe that the jump was worth it. I'm still believing that in all of this there is a lesson and something to grow from; some lesson I can take into my next but right now I'm sitting in the food bank trying not to let it define me. Remembering how we used to stand in line at various churches when I was growing up to get government cheese and peanut butter. Remembering how embarrassed I was standing in those lines, but also how much I loved making grilled cheese with that government cheese and peanut butter cookies with that government peanut butter. I never really wanted this life and in fact, until I jumped this was not my life. I spent years working in various jobs so that I didn't have to live this life. I spent years learning my field and being the model employee so that I wouldn't have to do this and yet today here I am. It's hard to describe how I feel about it.

When I arrived, I expected to walk in, grab some food and be on my way. Instead, I was met with a waiting room full of people looking at me as if I didn't belong, probably because I looked like I didn't belong there. Truthfully, I hadn't really looked at anyone there I just saw people and wanted to run like a scared puppy. What would these people think if they knew my books are releasing today but I needed to come to the food bank, and I had an eviction notice? It just felt like an oxymoron to me. I stood waiting for someone to be rude to me at the front desk, but no one was. I was surprised that everyone was nice and ready to help. I let my guard down some. As I waited to be called, my friend Jayme called me and when

I told her where I was, she said, "been there and it doesn't define you. It just helps you to identify with the people you are going to help." She always has an amazing way to look at things. I agreed and continued to wait. When the nice gentleman finally called my name, he took me back to the shopping area and on the way, he told me he knew someone whose name was the same as mine but hers was spelled, Laila. I said that I hadn't heard of that spelling. We went through the shopping section and he politely called off how many from each section we passed. One bread, one cereal, one meat from each bin, etc... etc., and as I gathered our needs, I wondered...how do people live on this and I've got to do something. There must be a way to do better. Now, that I'm home I wonder was that experience needed so that I can assist people with more than just the necessity. I don't believe God ever gives us a circumstance for nothing. There isn't anything that happens that we don't learn from but what is it for me in this day, this moment, this season. That's my confession today, I'm a jumper and today I needed the food bank but I'm sure it was not just for me.

I left the food bank with a purpose and a mission to help others in similar situations get better and be better. I was still embarrassed and still had an eviction notice, but I also left the food bank with information that could possibly help me get our back rent paid. If I could get the organizations to help us, I believed that I could take it from there, I just needed help getting caught up.

I spent the next few days calling the organizations trying to get help with the rent and electric and I also spoke with my car lender throughout January. I was not worried about the cable because that was a luxury and we could get back to it later. I called and talked to several organizations, but none of them could help me with the past rent because I had no concrete on paper way to prove I would be able to pay the rent afterwards. There were still other options, but we were slated to be out of our home by February 17th if the back rent was not paid and the organizations that may have been able to help, were unable to see me before that date. I felt that I did everything I knew to do including seeking greater wisdom and understanding, but I felt like I was losing everything.

In the days leading up to the date we were supposed to move out, I searched for an apartment hoping that if I could not get help with the back rent, I could try to at least get us another place to live so that we would not be on the street. I had no idea how I would pay for a new place, but I had to do something. I drove all around town looking for an apartment, but I continuously came up empty-handed. I was not willing to give up and I was not willing to lose my place either; I knew that there had to be a miracle coming.

As the date we were to move out got closer, I realized that we actually might lose our place and I needed to be ready. I also started having nightmares about losing my car and I would wake up stressed and afraid. I am sure that I could have gone back to work at this point, but I knew that was not what I was supposed to do. A week before we were scheduled to move out of our apartment, I saw Malachi off to school and went into my devotion time. I had begun a practice of looking out the window to see if my car was still there and that morning was no different. My truck was there, and I was thankful for another day with my truck especially since I had some things I needed to do that day.

As I went into my time with the Lord, I knew something was happening simultaneously, but I did not know what was happening. I felt such a loss but I was not upset or dismayed. After my time with the Lord, I went to my room to get ready to go to my appointment and when I looked out of the window, my truck was gone and I knew that was what I felt during my time of devotion. I did not have time to stop and grieve the truck because I had an appointment I needed to get to, but I was devastated. I took a cab to my appointment and when I was done, I took the bus back home.

A week later – 7 days to be exact, I was moving out of my home. I lost my home and car within a 7-day span and I honestly could no longer fight. Whatever God was going to do, He was not going to save our home and car, but I still had to believe that this was part of His full plan for my life. My son was devastated and so was I. I knew that I heard God right, but this just felt like I missed Him in some horrible way.

A few days before our move-out date, one of my close friends said Malachi and I could move in with her and her family. I did not respond to her because I really did not want to believe it was happening and I really did not want to lose my home. I also did not want to move in with anyone – I wanted my own place. When I finally realized that I was not going to be able to keep my place, I reluctantly agreed to move in with my friend and her family. It was such a hard choice for me to make, but it really was not a choice because I had no choice. There was nowhere else to go in Connecticut and while I could have moved back to New Jersey with my family, going back to New Jersey was not a viable option for us.

While I was shattered, grieved, and devastated that I lost my car and was now losing my place, I was certain that I heard God; certain that He directed me to leave; certain that He had been providing for us daily; certain that God was still taking care of us but I just did not understand this loss. I still trusted God's plan, but this was not what I wanted or expected. I could not figure out what I had done wrong and God seemed to be silent to my pleas to restore what I lost.

It was hard to verbalize how I felt, and I knew that people had their own opinions about what was happening and why. I knew that some thought I just needed to get a job and move on, so I recognized that I could not tell everyone everything. I also realized that I needed to seek the Lord for myself and hear Him on this situation for myself. I learned that not everyone had the same measure of faith and while I wanted to entrust my feelings, emotions, fears, and cares to those closest to me, I understood that it was unfair to place the burden of my faith on the shoulders of those who were unprepared and/or ill-equipped to handle it. So, I kept quiet, stayed to myself, and continued to pray. I trusted God because I knew that there had to be a plan, I just did not know what it was in full.

Malachi was absolutely devastated when we lost our home. The car he could do without but losing our home meant losing his friends, changing schools entirely and he was not happy. He tried to be a good sport about everything, but I could tell this whole thing devastated him. But as always, he tried to be strong for me – his Momma Bear, but I knew this really hurt him probably more than it was hurting me.

When we moved in with my friend, God spoke to me and He told me that this move was about an assignment. The Lord wanted me to be in this place for a purpose and as much as I loved my friend, I did not want the assignment. I did not want to be disobedient and I completely understood the importance of the assignment, but I wanted my home and car back not another assignment. I wanted God to show up and provide as He promised. I wanted Him to move mountains for me like He promised so that we could stay in our home. I was hurt, devastated, depressed, and on the verge of not caring, but there was something that kept me going forward despite what was happening around me. In my daze and anger, I knew that God had a bigger plan but all I wanted was what I lost.

I decided to take on the assignment the Lord gave me, and I gave it my all. It was my goal to fulfill the assignment and do whatever He told me to do and say what He told me to say. What He told me to do and what He told me to say was not always met with the welcome I thought it would be, but I trusted God and His voice alone. I also knew that God was doing something through me that He could not do through or with anyone else, so I pushed through. Day by day, I pressed through and I prayed. I pressed through and I prayed.

As time went on, Malachi and I grew closer, and once again we were connecting in a way that we had not been able to in our home. Not because I did not want to, but because his choices – friends, music, etc. - served as a block. It was like I'd say go left and he'd go right. I would say go here and he would go there. I did not like his friends or his taste in music and it was not just because I did not like it, but I could see that both were bad for him. Months before I left my job, I started to pray for him specifically regarding his friends. I prayed and specifically asked

God to move all the negative influences from his life and sure enough, that is exactly what He did when He uprooted us from our home. The friends who were taking him down the wrong path seemed to forget all about him once we moved and I was thankful yet hurting for him because I know how hard it was for him to make friends. But as heartbroken as he was about his friends, I was finally starting to see the light in his eyes that I missed when he was hanging with them. It was almost as if this had to happen to get him away from those influences because he could not hear me at all with those friends in his ear.

Once we got settled in at our friends' home, we spent more time talking and less time arguing (well I spent less time yelling). He even started voluntarily hugging me again, which he had stopped completely when we were living in our home. It was like I was finally getting my son back and I couldn't have been happier.

I soon began to realize that while I had lost my home and my car, I still had everything I needed, and my son still had everything he needed. I learned that what I thought were needs in my life, were not always needs. We had food, a place to live, and every day God was speaking. He spoke to me in prayer time, on the bus, while I was driving (when my friend would let me use her car), and even while I was walking. God's voice was never far from me and while it was uncomfortable, I trusted in God's plan.

| 4 |

One Word from God Can Change Everything

After living in my friend's home for almost three months, I needed a break. It wasn't bad where we were, but the stress of losing my house and my car was starting to get the best of me. I needed to get away so I could breathe. When I wasn't working, I was still volunteering at church, and I had also picked up a website design client. My days were full; I was tired and ready to decompress.

Fortunately, I was invited to attend a Christian business conference in Virginia Beach in April. I was excited, remembering the training from the year before. I did not have the funds to travel, but I believed that God would make a way – and He did. The conference host reached out to me and told me that a generous donor paid for my ticket to the conference, my hotel room, and a $100.00 credit towards my transportation. I was so thankful and excited; going to this conference would be a welcome interruption to my new normal.

The $100 credit was not enough for a plane ticket or a rental car, so I decided to take the train to Virginia. The train ride was more than 11 hours, and I loved every minute of it. It was the first time since my trip to Florida the year before that I enjoyed quality time alone. When I went to the conference the year before, I went with three other women, and while I thought we would make the trip a tradition, God had other plans.

When it came time for the 2016 conference, each woman who traveled with me the year before was unable to attend. But like everything that was taking place for me in this season, it was purposeful. God needed my undivided attention. It was clear that this year's conference was simply about Him and me.

When I arrived at the hotel in Virginia, I was excited about the conference and what God would say to me. I checked in and headed up to my room with my luggage. When I arrived in the room, I was in awe. The room was beautiful, with a fantastic view of the ocean. When I opened the door to the balcony, the sounds of the beach showered over me like a warm breeze – the waves hitting the shore, the birds, the breeze cool air – it was so much to take it in, and I was mesmerized. I loved being near the water, so this was exactly where I needed to be.

The conference was a total of three days, and there were speakers during each session. Each day, God spoke through anointed speakers and psalmists. Each session was better than the last and each speaker was powerful. The Lord even showed up during our lunch breaks – it was amazing!

Not only did God speak to me but He healed me that weekend as well. He healed so much of the hurt from the past that was lingering in my heart, mind, and soul. As much as I wanted to go with other people, this time was what I needed. I needed God to let me know that despite everything, He had not forgotten about me. I needed Him to remind me that the promises He made to me were still valid. I needed to hear Him clearly without distractions, and that is exactly what happened.

During one of the sessions, I heard a loud voice say to me clearly and boldly, "MOVE." It was so loud that I thought someone was asking me to move. But I looked around, and everyone else was focused on the speaker. I knew at that moment that it was God who spoke, but I had no idea what MOVE meant so I wrote down what He said in my journal and purposed to pray about what I heard.

So, when I returned from my trip, I focused my prayer on that one word – MOVE – it was all I could think about. What was the thing God wanted me to do? I prayed and asked God for more details. He didn't answer right away, but what He did do, was start making things uncomfortable again. I realized that this was God's sign of movement for me – feeling uncomfortable in what were once comfortable surroundings.

One day while I was driving my friend's car to church, I asked God where He wanted me to go, and He answered clearly, "Minnesota." This response didn't catch me completely by surprise. In the years before God gave me this directive, He had shown me Minnesota in the craziest places – on movies, license plates, TV shows. It seemed like everywhere I went, I saw or heard Minnesota. In fact, I had even suspected I would move to Minnesota at some point. I just had no idea it would be so soon.

So when God told me that He wanted me to move to Minnesota now, I had a Sarah moment – I laughed! I was not laughing at God. I was laughing because the thought of packing up and moving to Minnesota was hysterical to me. That was not the instruction I was expecting at all.

After I finished laughing, I told God that if He really wanted me to move to Minnesota, I would go, but He needed to provide the flight. I wasn't negotiating with God or demanding anything from Him. I was believing Him to provide what I needed to do His will. I knew that if God wanted me to be someplace, He would make a way for me to get there. I asked Him when I was to leave, and the first date he gave me was June 1st. I was petrified. June 1st was only a few weeks away and I had no idea how I was supposed to uproot my entire life by then.

I only told a few people what God had instructed me to do because I knew not everyone would understand. If I'm honest, I didn't fully understand and I had my own moments of doubt. So, I didn't want or need any more doubt because I was wobbling enough already. I was afraid to confide in someone whose faithlessness would pull me down more.

I needed people who could help me stand in faith especially with the magnitude of this request.

One of the people I told about my journey offered to buy my airline ticket for me when I was ready to go. God opened the door and answered my prayer by sending someone to purchase the flight. But the closer I got to my move date, the more fear gripped me, and in the end, June 1st came and went and I was still in Connecticut, unable to shake the fear of yet another jump. But my fear did not change God's mind; His instructions remained the same. Move to Minnesota. My faith would have to rise to the occasion because God's direction was clear.

The Lord gave me a new move date of August 31st and I knew that this was all or nothing. I had to be out of Connecticut by August 31st. As scared as I was to leave everything I knew to go to a city I knew nothing about, I knew that God needed me in Minnesota.

After getting the new date to move, I told the same sister who offered to purchase my flight for the June 1st move date, I would be moving on August 31st. She said she was still willing to pay for my flight, but she wanted to make sure I had what I needed when I got to Minnesota. I told her God would take care of me.

That evening, we went online to buy my airline ticket to Minnesota. As I searched for a flight, we talked about what I was going to do with Malachi and where I would live. She was happy for me, but we were both nervous. She asked me if I was sure I was doing the right thing, and although my nerves were on edge, I assured her I was. I knew God was sending me to Minnesota. I just didn't know much more than that.

She gave me her card information and looked at me as I entered the numbers. She said matter-of-factly, "Well, once you hit that button, you can't back out." She was right. I knew that once the flight was purchased, my life would change forever. I also knew I had to do it. I had postponed the move once already. I would not be disobedient again. I was afraid, but I did it. I checked out and watched as the computer processed her card. It went through, and I was on the clock. I had just over a month to get my life in order and get to Minnesota.

I only knew of two people in Minnesota, but I didn't know either of them well enough to say they would let me live with them until I got settled. I had never been to the state, but I knew it was cold – bitter cold at times – and it was home to some great musicians. That was the extent of my knowledge. As I look back on it, I realize that God had given me dreams about Minnesota long before He told me I would be moving. I just didn't know how to interpret them at the time.

When I told my son, Malachi, the Lord wanted me to move to Minnesota, he made it very clear he did not want to come with me. He was about to enter his senior year of high school, and he had already had to switch schools one time when we lost our home. Malachi was done with moving, so I began praying about where he could stay. I knew that our living situation at the time would not work for him alone, but the friends who I thought might be willing to take him in lived outside of his school district. I only knew of a few people in our area who would consider keeping Malachi for me. I knew it was a longshot, but I decided to ask if he could stay with them. I prayed that someone I trusted would be kind enough to let him stay until the school year was complete.

I realized it was a huge responsibility to take on for anyone, but I had to try. I knew of family members and friends who'd taken in other people's children for a plethora of reasons, so I was prayerful someone in our circle could help.

| 5 |

Fly Liela-Beans Fly

A month before I was slated to move to Minnesota, I started praying with my friend, Rachel. We were both in desperate need for God to move in our lives before the end of the summer. She was in North Carolina, and I was in Connecticut, but our need for God brought us together on the phone every morning at 7 am. We were both facing tough situations, and we needed answers by the end of August.

As we prayed together every day, God began to answer us in unexpected ways. His answers started on the inside of our hearts and souls. He brought to light issues like past hurts, unforgiveness, ungodly soul ties, and more. As we prayed, God delivered us trauma by trauma. We were both stunned at the amount of healing we had to endure, but as we trusted and obeyed God, He started opening doors for us in unique ways.

As we got closer to the end of the summer and my departure to Minnesota, it became clear that none of my friends in Connecticut would be able to keep Malachi. Despite his strong desire to stay in Connecticut, I had no choice but to take him with me. When I told him he would have to go with me, he was extremely upset. I won't lie; I was hurt too. But I knew it was a huge responsibility to take care of someone else's child, even if he was 18. We had hoped for a different outcome, but I understood.

Now that Malachi would be coming with me, my thoughts regarding Minnesota had to include both of us. I needed to get him on the same flight I was on, but with just days to our planned departure, that wasn't going to be easy or cheap. I also needed a place for us to sleep. I honestly had not thought much about where I would sleep when I was planning to go to Minnesota alone. I was happy just to obey God and see where He would lead. I didn't know if God would send someone to the airport to pick me up and provide room and board or if I would go to a shelter. I didn't know, and until I had to consider Malachi, I was ok with whatever God decided. But now that my son would be with me, I asked God for the next steps.

The one person that I talked to in Minnesota let me know ahead of time that she did not have room for Malachi and me, but she promised to help us in any way she could. As I prayed, God told me to book a hotel for seven days. So, I looked for hotel accommodations that included breakfast, so at least we'd have a good meal every morning. I booked the LaQuinta Hotel for seven nights, not knowing how I would pay for the room. The card I used to secure the room was almost at the limit, and I didn't have much cash on hand. But God said book the room, so I did it. I'd let Him decide how the bill would be paid. With our first week's accommodations set, I focused on getting Malachi on the same flight with me.

My flight left Connecticut in the afternoon on August 31st, and while I knew I could call and change my flight, it would cost me money I didn't have. Besides, August 31st was the date God had given me. He knew I would have to take Malachi with me when He gave me the date. So, it made sense that He would make a way for us to go together.

The tickets for the flight I had booked were now well over $300. I did not even have half of that. My prayer partner, Rachel, and I prayed together for Malachi's flight. We also prayed for the hotel funds and all that she needed to have before the summer ended. We were both on the verge of great things, but we could not see how the things we needed would happen, so we set up an emergency call with our prayer mentor. We had just days left before Malachi and I were supposed to leave for Minnesota and there was still so much that needed to be done. I still did not have Malachi's ticket and I still had no clue how I was going to pay for the hotel let alone how we were going to eat when we arrived in Minnesota.

As I waited for the call with our prayer mentor, I received a call from the same person who purchased my airline ticket. She asked me if I was able to find a place for Malachi to stay. I told her that he would need to come with me, but I couldn't purchase his ticket yet. She said we could try using her credit card again. She said she was not sure if there was enough on her card, but we could try.

I logged onto the airline's website, added Malachi's flight to my cart, and proceeded to checkout using the information she provided to me. As the website buffered, I held my breath. A message I had never seen before popped up on the screen. I told my friend there was an error, but it wasn't a decline message. She told me to try it again, and this time the transaction went through.

We both breathed a sigh of relief. I could not believe it; I had Malachi's ticket with literally just hours to go. I called my prayer partner and told her what happened, and we rejoiced together. However, there were still obstacles in our path, so we were anxious to get on our call with our mentor.

When it was time for our call, we told our prayer mentor what was happening - the breakthroughs we were receiving and the challenges we still had left. When we finished, we waited for some bombshell prophetic word or some new wisdom, but she simply said, "You don't need me. You got this!"

Rachel and I were panicked because we were at the end of the summer and needed a breakthrough. But our mentor began to recount what we had told her about how God had already moved. Listening to her, we were encouraged and gained confidence that God would continue working on our behalf. Our prayer mentor decreed and declared that we would receive what we had been praying for, and she said that she looked forward to our testimonies.

The days leading up to our departure, we spent our days packing up our lives in Connecticut and saying goodbyes to our friends. I still couldn't believe we would be moving to Minnesota. I was a bag of emotions – sometimes excited and sometimes nervous but still concerned about Malachi because, for him, this whole move was not what he wanted.

****

When we arrived at the airport, Malachi was finally starting to show some signs of excitement. I thanked God that he had begun to come around. After we checked our bags and made it through security, we had time to have a meal together. We ate pizza, talked about our trip, and for the first time since I brought up moving to Minnesota, he smiled and laughed. That laughter unlocked a breath in me I didn't know I was holding. My heart beamed with joy!

When we boarded our flight, I began to pray because I still did not have enough to pay for our hotel. I sat in my seat next to Malachi, excited yet petrified. As he looked out the window, I prayed in my heavenly language. I prayed throughout both legs of our flight, believing that God would do something, send someone, or somehow bless us with the funds for the hotel He told me to book.

For me, faith is not magic. Faith is hard to explain practically. It's supposed to be that way. Faith is strange to those unfamiliar with it. Living by faith often appears strange, radical, crazy, and unnatural, but it was how I had decided to live my life. My belief that God would provide the hotel and the funds we needed to eat was not because I did not plan. He was my plan. During my preparation and prayer time, the Lord reminded me how He sent Abraham out in Genesis 12. Abraham did not know where God was sending him. He did not have a plan; he simply went where God told him to go. That is what faith is.

When God told me to move to Minnesota, He was my plan, and He was responsible for taking care of us. God continually confirmed His word concerning my move through various trusted sources. It was clear to me and to those I trusted spiritually that God was with me and that Minnesota was where He wanted me to be.

When we arrived in Minnesota, the woman I had met online, Jackie, met us at the airport. Jackie and I were part of the same Christian business group on Facebook. When I was preparing to move to Minnesota, the group's founder suggested I reach out to Jackie because she lived in Minnesota. When we arrived at the airport, Jackie was waiting for us, and she offered to take us to our hotel. I was relieved to see a friendly face.

Jackie drove us to the LaQuinta hotel closest to the airport. When we arrived, we took our luggage out of the car and headed into the hotel. As we were standing at the front desk waiting for the hotel clerk to find our reservation, Jackie asked if she could pay for 2 of our hotel nights. My eyes filled with tears. The hotel clerk started speaking to me, but I was too overwhelmed to hear what she said. I finally composed myself enough to talk to the hotel clerk, and she told me that we were at the wrong hotel. So we all got back in Jackie's car with all our luggage and proceeded to the right hotel.

When we arrived at the right LaQuinta, just a few miles from the airport, we unloaded Jackie's car and went into the hotel. I asked the front desk clerk, Eric if we were at the right LaQuinta, and this time we were. I was tired and hungry, but I was thankful Jackie had offered to pay for our first two nights. When Eric pulled up our reservation for the week, he asked me how I would like to pay. Since Jackie was paying for two nights, my immediate thought was to pay for those nights first and then trust God for the balance. But Eric informed us that I needed to pay for the week upfront. I had no clue what I was going to do.

Jackie asked me if I had the money, and I told her I did not but I was trusting God for it. We moved to the side so Eric could help other guests, and we began to pray. I didn't know what else to do. I had obeyed all of the instructions God had given me, so I waited to see what He would do next.

A few short moments later, Jackie told me she would pay for the entire week for us. She just needed to go home to get her credit card. I was a ball of emotions. On the one hand, I was happy God provided, but on the other hand, I wanted to be sure she would have enough for her family. Hesitantly, I asked if she was sure. Jackie was adamant that God would work it out.

As Jackie left to get her card, fear started to creep in, and worry tried to overtake me. Thoughts like "what if she doesn't come back?" or "what if she can't do it?" The fears that came up reminded me that I did not know her well, and the room was a lot of money, so maybe she would not come back and pay for the room. I've had people offer to help me in the past only to have them not show up with what was needed, but right amid my angst, the Lord said one word to me – **TRUST**. I knew at that moment that I could breathe, go and have dinner with Malachi, and trust Jackie to come back.

Malachi and I walked over to a nearby restaurant named Culver's for dinner. We were both jittery and excited, so we chatted a lot about our new state. I decided not to tell our family that we moved, so we talked about what we thought our family members might say. As we ate, we both fell in love with Culver's cheese curds. Neither of us had ever had cheese curds before, but they were so good. Malachi asked me if I thought they were hiring, and I told him I didn't know, but he would probably spend his paycheck on cheese curds. We both laughed because we knew it was true. It felt good to sit with him and laugh about silly stuff. As much as fear was trying to creep in, God's peace covered us, and that was all I needed.

When we finished eating, we went back over to the hotel to wait for Jackie, and just like she promised, she returned, paid for the room, and helped us up to the room with our bags. She told me she would check on us the next day and told me to get some rest. Once we settled into the room, the emotions bubbled over again – I was crying, yet so happy and thankful. I obeyed God, got on the flight he provided, booked the hotel like He said, and we were now sitting safely in a hotel room in Minnesota. The Lord provided for us each step of the way. My spirit was invigorated, but my body was exhausted. I called my prayer partner to fill her in on the day's events, took a shower, and we were both asleep before we knew it.

The next day my prayer partner and I prayed together in the morning, and our first week in Minnesota began. I was excited to see more of our new state. I was also excited about an interview I scheduled later in the week. Before we left Connecticut, I looked for a job in Minnesota and I had several phone interviews. One of those phone interviews went so well, I was asked to come in for an in-person interview. The employer and I had a great rapport, so to me, the interview was just a formality. I was excited to be starting a new job soon after arriving in Minnesota and felt like it would not be long before we were living in our own home once again.

After breakfast, I sent my Bishop a text message and told him that we made it to Minnesota. I also told him how God provided for our hotel room for the week. Then Malachi and I walked to Walmart to get a few things that we needed. As we walked, I felt peace. I couldn't really describe it, but even though we were staying in a hotel and I was unsure of where we were going next I was at peace.

As we walked and talked, we noticed the stores and shops that were different. We also noticed that there were traffic lights on the onramp to the highway and I could not figure out why. It was so weird because I always knew the onramp to be the acceleration lane so it didn't make sense to have a traffic light there. Since I couldn't figure it out, I made a mental note to ask Jackie about it the next time she came to pick us up.

While we were at Walmart, my Bishop sent me back a text letting me know that he was proud of me and that he was happy God had moved for us. He ended his text by saying, "Fly, Liela-Beans, Fly," and I knew just what He meant. I had jumped when I left the law firm, but now I was flying. I was soaring in faith, and he wanted me to continue trusting God and obeying despite all odds. His text message motivated me to continue moving forward boldly, even when it didn't make sense to natural eyes.

After we arrived back at the hotel, we stopped at Culver's to get something to eat. We were both big fans of Culver's cheese curds and the fact that it was in the same parking lot as our hotel only made it better. In our downtime in the hotel, we looked for work and a place to stay long-term.

I continued daily prayers alone and with my prayer partner that first week. While I was thankful that God moved us safely, we still had needs that only God could fill. I also spent time with Jackie; she took us anywhere we needed to go that first week. Jackie was a blessing. I wanted new Godly friends, and God provided one in her. We were still getting to know one another, but she went out of her way to make sure we had everything we needed every day.

The week seemed to crawl by for us as I worked to find a home, secure a job, and get Malachi in school. On Friday, I woke up excited for my job interview. I knew that I had it in the bag. It was just a matter of meeting my soon-to-be new boss face to face. In my head, I thought once I officially secured this position, it would not be much longer before I could get a place for Malachi and me.

Jackie offered to drive me to my interview and bring me back to the hotel afterward. I did a phone interview for this position before I left Connecticut, and I got the impression that the face-to-face interview was simply a formality. When I walked into the building, gospel music played at the front desk, and I took that as a sign from God that the job was mine. The interviewer met me in the lobby, and we had a great conversation. It did not feel like an interview; in fact, it felt like two old friends reconnecting for the first time.

After our conversation, the interviewer brought the company's CEO into our meeting, and we also had a wonderful conversation. I knew then that the job was mine. I walked out of the interview with a promise that I would hear back from my interviewer on Tuesday to formally offer me the position. I was so excited because the company appeared to be just what I needed, and it was exactly the position I wanted.

On Sunday, we went to church with Jackie and her children. Jackie's church was small but friendly. In fact, I found that most people in Minnesota seemed friendlier and there was even a term for it – Minnesota Nice. We had a good time in service, it was different from my home church, and while I was longing for the experience of my home church, I was thankful to be in the house of the Lord.

After service was over, I asked Jackie's Pastor, Pastor Carey, to pray for us because we only had a couple more days in the hotel, and I needed God to move for us. I expected to have a job starting on Tuesday, but we would need resources to live until I received my first paycheck.

After he prayed for us, I felt better, and I knew God would make a way. We left the church, and Jackie took us to the grocery store and paid for our dinner. I was not expecting her to do that, but I was thankful that she blessed us. When we got back to the hotel, Malachi and I rested.

I believed Tuesday was going to be a big day for me. First, I was supposed to get the call from the company I interviewed with formally offering me the position and letting me know when I could start. Second, I was going to see a house that I found online a few weeks before I left Connecticut. I'd been praying about for weeks. My faith was energized, and I was prayerful that the Lord would provide the funds we needed for this house, although I had no clue how that would happen. At that point, I believed God could do anything, and honestly, I still believe that.

I was excited to get the job and the home; I never dreamed I would end Tuesday disappointed on both accounts. But that is precisely what happened. Tuesday came, and Jackie and I drove out to the house I'd found. The realtor showed us around, and everything I thought I loved about the place – the water view, the office, the kitchen – ended up being lackluster. The water view was more of a swamp view, and the house had a condo on top of it that belonged to someone else. I was deflated because it was not what I expected at all. I tried to make it work in my head, and I kept a smile on my face, but in my heart, I knew that despite my desire for this home to be mine, it was not what I wanted.

Jackie and I drove back to the hotel and discussed the house's possibilities, but I was significantly less enthusiastic about the house than I had been before we viewed it. I went back to the hotel and waited to hear from the job. 5 pm came, and there was nothing. I thought maybe she just got busy, or perhaps there had been an emergency. I tried to be positive, but the call I was expecting letting me know I had the job never came.

My faith was being tested, and fear was growing. We had to be out of the hotel the next day, and I had no clue what we would do. During our seven days at the hotel, God had provided funds, but the money we received was not enough to cover another week at the LaQuinta. But I still believed. I was praying with my prayer partner every day, and I just knew God would move by Wednesday morning.

I woke up Wednesday morning nervous, anxious, and afraid. My prayer partner and I prayed together that morning as usual. I was scared, but I knew God to move mightily for us. Later that morning, another friend reached out to me and agreed with me in prayer for more time at the hotel. By this time, it was almost noon, so I called the front desk and asked about late checkout. Late checkout was at 2 pm, so they allowed us to stay until then.

As I talked with my friend, he suggested sitting in the lobby and waiting for God to move. I heard him, but I was in full panic mode because I had no idea where we were going to go. I cried and told God I could not believe He brought us all the way to Minnesota just to leave us stranded. I knew that He wouldn't do that but at the moment, I could not stop myself from being overcome with fear. We packed our things with no idea where we were going.

This was a new level of faith for me. There was nothing I could do to make this work on my own. I did not have enough money to stay at the LaQuinta, and I did not have enough money to go to another hotel. I was helpless to do anything for myself; I needed God to move on our behalf.

I sent a text to Jackie to let her know I was unsure where we were going to go, and she told me that she was on her way to the hotel. When she arrived at the hotel, she came up to the room and said she had an idea. Jackie had enough money for another week at the LaQuinta, or she could use her Marriot Rewards points to get us a different room if we found one.

I could feel myself breathe when she provided the options to me. It was like I had been holding my breath all morning, waiting to see how God was going to move. When Jackie said she would help us again, my lungs could finally relax. Jackie told me that God had spoken to her on the way over and told her to help me. She said God reminded her of the points she had in her account from some traveling she had done years before and she was willing to share them with us so we could get another hotel room.

I was so thankful God spoke to her and instructed her to help us with another hotel stay. She stood in our LaQuinta hotel room browsing local Marriott hotels on her phone while Malachi and I finished packing up. When we were done, she booked us five nights at the TownePlace and Suites in Eden Prairie. We packed up her car and headed over to our new place. I was so thankful and the weight of the panic that I had just hours earlier was gone. I could breathe and rest without panic.

| 6 |

Stretching Our Wings

When we arrived at the TownPlace wasn't as afraid anymore about Jackie taking care of the bill. She had already proven herself to be a loyal friend. Even though we'd only just met. I was confident that her desire to help us was from a place of care and concern. And I knew that God sent her, and I was thankful. The hotel had free breakfast along with a full kitchen in the room. There were only one queen bed and a pull-out couch in the room for sleep, but the room also had a separate office with a TV. Malachi was not happy about the pull-out couch, but he sucked it up as soon as he realized he could play his game and not have to share a TV with me. While Malachi was thankful not to have to share a TV with me, I was thankful that I did not have to go outside to pray with my prayer partner in the mornings as I could just come into the office and pray without disturbing Malachi's sleep.

I was so thankful that the Lord had come through for us and provided for us again. Once we were settled, in our hotel room, I felt myself breathe just a little more. I hoped that this would be the last hotel we'd stay in or at the very least I would have a job and be able to pay for our own hotel. It has never been my bend to depend on other people. Before this journey began, I was accustomed to taking care of my responsibilities on my own, and that included housing. I did not like depending on others, but this was a new season for me and it was as if God wanted me to rely on Him solely. I was beginning to realize in this season that He moved when He wanted and how He wanted, using whom He chose to help us. It was such an odd juxtaposition.

Once we were settled at the Town Place hotel, I walked across the street to the supermarket to get groceries so I could make dinner for us. Since this room had a full kitchen, I could make dinner without using a microwave, and as crazy as it sounds, that excited me. We'd only been in Minnesota a week, but I was already tired of eating out. Once I got what we needed, I walked back to the hotel and I realized where I was.

Before we moved to Minnesota, there were a few towns I researched because I wanted to learn more and Eden Prairie was one of them. I discovered that it was a great town with a good school system, and as I walked back to the hotel that day Eden Prairie felt like home. I know it sounds odd because we'd only just arrived and I'd only walked from the hotel to the supermarket, but there was something more to this place and I knew it was for us.

When I got back to the hotel, I was thankful and after dinner, I sat at the desk and searched for work while Malachi played his game. I scoured internet job sites looking for work and a place to live. I knew that I had 5 nights and 6 days until we had to leave this hotel and I did not want to have another experience of not knowing where we were going to end up. The problem was I had no money and no job to secure a home and I was not sure how we were going to get a home, but I knew we could not live in a hotel forever.

The next day, I started the process of enrolling Malachi into school, so that he could start his senior year of high school. Even though I did not know where we were going to live, I knew that he needed to be in school. I hated that he was having to start over at a new school especially for his senior year, but I knew that Eden Prairie was one of the best school districts in Minnesota, so that helped to ease some of my concern. When I called the school district, the administrator that I spoke with was very kind and provided me with all of the steps I needed to make sure that he could get started with school. We soon had a meeting with a counselor at the school so that he could get signed up for classes and start school.

When we arrived at the school and walked in, the school was massive and it was the kind of school I was always dreamed my child would go to, but Malachi was not really as excited as I was and I understood. I knew that it was hard to leave not one but two schools and two sets of friends. I could not imagine what it was like to be in his shoes, so I prayed. I always wanted him to attend one school for all four years of high school like I did, but God had other plans. The truth was that had God not intervened in our lives, we'd still be in Connecticut and he'd still be hanging with the wrong crowd and who knows how that would have ended up, but I was thankful for a change even though it was challenging. I was also thankful for the opportunity to experience God in a new way and I knew Minnesota was where we needed to be.

As much uncertainty as I faced about where we were going to go or what we were going to do when the 5 nights were up, we did take the time to enjoy our surroundings. The hotel was within walking distance of a mall and a few other stores. A few days after we arrived at the hotel, Malachi and I walked to the mall, Eden Prairie Center, one afternoon just to get out of the hotel and see the neighborhood. I was excited to be in a new place, not just the hotel but I was excited to be starting my life in Minnesota.

I applied for numerous jobs while we were staying at the TownPlace including a job at Best Buy. I knew that I wanted to work there as soon as I saw their headquarters off the highway. When I saw the job online I applied almost immediately and prayed I would hear back quickly. I also applied for other IT positions that were available in the area, and I received some callbacks and a couple of phone interviews, but no face-to-face interviews.

As I waited for word from positions I applied for, I kept myself busy with client projects that I started working on before I left Connecticut. Between looking for a job, client projects and looking for a place it felt like I was working, and it felt good. I hoped with all that was in me that by the time the week was over, I would have a job or enough money to stay in this hotel another week. While I kept myself busy with client projects and job hunting, Malachi played his game and looked for work as well.

As we got closer to the end of our time at the TownPlace, panic started to creep into my thoughts again, but this time the panic did not overtake me. I prayed every day and asked God to move for us because we needed Him. I still did not have a clear path to employment despite my best efforts, but I still believed God. I didn't know where we were going to go, but I knew I had to trust God to provide.

| 7 |

Gaining Strength

Tuesday came, and it was time for us to move again. Once again, I was unsure where we were going to go. But unlike the week before, I was not distraught and crying like crazy. I was still on edge because I did not know our next step, but I was definitely more composed.

After we picked Malachi up from school, Jackie and I strategized and decided I would use the points I earned from our week-long stay at our first hotel, the LaQuinta, to book another stay at a different LaQuinta. With my points, I booked two nights for Malachi and me for less than $17. After that, Jackie used the remaining balance of her Marriott points to book us another room. It was a little piecemeal, but we had a plan for the next week. I was thankful.

When we arrived at the LaQuinta in Minnetonka, we checked in and put our luggage in the room. Then Jackie took us to the store to get dinner. Jackie offered to pay for our dinner and anything else we needed. We opted for pantry-type ready-to-eat items since there was no refrigerator or microwave in our room.

When we arrived back at the hotel, Jackie said she would come by in the morning and take Malachi to school. She also volunteered to pick him up when school was over. I knew that was a sacrifice for her, but I did not know where we were, and I had no idea how I would get him to school on my own.

While Malachi was at school, I looked for both a job and a place to live. I also prayed. It was difficult looking for a place to stay because I had no idea where I was relative to Minneapolis and I also had no idea where I would be working. Still, I applied for different options with the thought I would get a car after I got a job, and we wouldn't be limited in our location.

While we were staying at the LaQuinta in Minnetonka, there was a hiring fair at the hotel, so I asked if I could apply. We were in our 3rd hotel, and I figured any job would be better than no job. It turned out that the job fair was not for the hotel but for the Ryder's Cup occurring in a couple of weeks in Chaska, Minnesota. I talked to the interviewer about the open positions, but I felt like those jobs were not for me. They were all vendor-related jobs that required a lot of investment for very little profit. There were other things that bothered me about the jobs that I can't explain, but I knew I was not supposed to apply for those jobs. I took the application anyway, but I knew God was letting me know that these jobs were not for me. The next day, I asked Jackie her opinion, and she confirmed those weren't the jobs for me because it was far out and there was not going to be a way for me to get there without a car. So, I continued my search for a job and prayed that I would get something soon.

Once we checked out of the LaQuinta hotel, Jackie and I picked up Malachi from school and headed to the TownPlace hotel in Eagan, where Jackie used her points to get us five nights. I was thankful I didn't have to worry about where we were going to go, but I was growing weary of moving around.

| 8 |

Growing in Faith

We checked into another TownPlace hotel on Wednesday, and since there was a bible study that evening, we put our things in the hotel and went to Jackie's house. On the way to her house, Jackie said she had a plan – I would drive her car to bible study, and she would use her mom's car so that I could take Malachi to school in the morning.

I was surprised at her offer and asked her several times if she was sure about the plan. She said she was, so I thankfully accepted. I followed Jackie to Sam's Club where she put gas in her car for me, gas in her Mom's car for her, and then she took us in to get pizza. I was willing to buy pizza for Malachi and me, but she insisted, so I thankfully accepted.

I realize that God was teaching me how to receive in that season, and He often used Jackie and others to help me learn the lesson. As crazy as it sounds, it was a lot harder for me to receive than it was for me to give. Receiving when you're in need requires humility. It requires vulnerability, and most of us don't like feeling exposed. But God says He meets us in that vulnerable place[1], so it's in our best interest for us to allow Him to teach us how to stay there.

As we left church that night, Malachi and I got in Jackie's car and drove to the hotel. The room at the TownPlace in Eagan was similar to the one in Eden Prairie, but everything was all in one room. There was a pull-out bed for Malachi, a queen-sized bed for me, and a desk and a chair. When we finally got back to the room (I had gotten a little lost on the way back), we ate, showered, and jumped in bed. We had to be up before the sun for me to get Malachi to school on time.

The next morning, I dropped Malachi at school and drove to Jackie's house so I could return her car. After I arrived at Jackie's house, she drove me back to the hotel and told me that she would pick up Malachi after school and drop him back at the hotel. She dropped off Malachi and left me her car so that I could get Malachi to school the next day. I was so thankful for Jackie's help. She was going above and beyond for us.

The next day I dropped Malachi at school, and to save gas, I brought my laptop with me so I could work at Starbucks. I applied for jobs, updated my blog, and created some images for a client project. While at Starbucks, I received a call back from Best Buy for an interview. I was elated. I scheduled the interview for the next week, and while I did not know where we would be staying at the time, I was determined to take advantage of this opportunity. I was ready to work and start making money, so Malachi and I could find a permanent place to live.

After picking Malachi up, I headed back to Jackie's house to take her car back. I told Jackie about the interview, and she was happy for me. We prayed for God's will concerning the job. Jackie took us back to the hotel, and since it was Friday, we stayed at the hotel until Sunday when Jackie picked us up for church.

I shopped enough during the week that we had plenty to eat over the weekend, but there was also a Chili's across from the hotel, and I really wanted to eat there after church on Sunday. I knew it was trivial, but I also knew God tells us to bring all of our concerns to Him, so I prayed, asking God to send me the money to go out to eat.[2] I know we could've done without eating at Chili's, but I wanted some normalcy, even if it was just for one night. I also prayed for the funds we needed for our next hotel. We were checking out of TownPlace on Monday, and again I was not sure where we would go.

On Sunday as we prepared for church, I received a phone call from a woman at my home church who had purchased a bed from me before I left Connecticut. When I'd realized that Malachi was coming with me, I sold her his twin bed in good faith. She didn't have the money to give to me right away, but she needed the bed, and I trusted she would pay me when she could. I didn't realize then that my good deed would come back to bless me. Just as I prayed for the Lord to provide me with funds for a meal out, she called, ready to pay her debt. She promised to send the money through a Walmart to Walmart transaction after church, and I marveled at God's provision.

After church, Pastor Carey came up to me, and we talked for a while. He told me that I reminded him of his mom and that the Lord had shown him some things about me. Pastor Carey described his mom as one who bore burdens – a woman who embodied superhuman strength. She tried to help everyone and rarely asked for anything in return. I cried because all of what he said was accurate of me. I am the type who rarely asks for help, and I am more of a listener than a talker.

If I have an issue, I keep it to myself unless it's a major problem. I don't want to burden others. Besides, experience had taught me not everyone cared to listen to my woes. I am usually the one people come to for wisdom and answers, not the other way around. They're familiar with a particular dynamic in our relationship. I don't hold that against them. However, being the perpetual problem solver can be exhausting. It can feel like no one sees you - like no one knows your heart. That Sunday afternoon, Pastor Carey, much like my Bishop in Connecticut, saw me, and I knew I could trust him.

As we continued to talk, he asked me about our living arrangements for the upcoming week. I told him I did not have a plan yet for where we would stay, but we would be checking out of the hotel on Monday. He told me to stay put, and when he came back, he handed me an envelope. I thanked him without looking in the envelope, and Jackie, Malachi, and I left.

After church, I received a text letting me know that the money from the bed sale was waiting for me at Walmart. Jackie allowed me to use her car again so that I could get Malachi to school the next day. We picked up the money from Walmart and enjoyed a lovely inexpensive meal at Chili's. While we were still in the car, I opened the envelope from Pastor Carey. It was a check for $250. That was enough for a few more nights at a hotel. God had shown Himself faithful again. Now I just needed to narrow down where we could go.

Despite my desire for this process of faith-walking to be over quickly, God was consistent in His provision. As much as I wanted the rollercoaster ride to end, I knew that God was with us and the proof was His daily provision. I didn't know what was ahead, but with an upcoming job interview at Best Buy, I was encouraged that we moving in the right direction.

| 9 |

Learning to Balance and Believe

The next day, Malachi and I got up early, packed up our things, and checked out of the TownPlace hotel. I made sure we took advantage of the hotel's free breakfast before we left, and then I drove Malachi to school. Once I dropped Malachi off, I went to Starbucks to wait for the school day to be over and also to find a new place for us to go that evening.

I had the money from the church, but hotel prices had begun to skyrocket because of the upcoming Ryder's Cup. Hotels that were normally $70 - $80 a night were now charging double that, and most places were already booked up. I kept searching, and the only option I thought would work was the Super 8 in Chaska, Minnesota. It was within my budget, and Malachi could get the Southwest Prime bus to pick him up at the hotel.

I became familiar with Southwest Prime while we were staying in Eden Prairie. It was an on-demand bus service that serviced Eden Prairie, Chanhassen, and Chaska. That area did not have a local bus service, so Southwest Prime served as public transportation. I was thankful that the service existed and took full advantage of it when we could.

When I picked Malachi up from school, we drove to the hotel to check-in and, I was mortified. The hotel was not in good condition at all. It smelled like dirty rugs and urine from the moment we walked in the door. I thought someone was playing a cruel joke on me, or maybe we were at the wrong place, but we weren't.

We walked into the office, and I realized that it also served as the breakfast area. It was also dirty; everything looked and felt dirty. I knew immediately I did not want to eat any of the breakfast they served. In fact, I did not want to stay there at all.

As I looked around and waited for someone to help us, I realized that the access doors to the rooms were left open and unlocked. Anybody could walk through to the rooms without being checked to see if they belonged there. It honestly felt like an hourly hotel, and I did not want to subject my son to that.

When the clerk came, I shared my concerns with him regarding safety and conditions, and he said I could call customer service and try to cancel my reservation. So, I got back in the car and called customer service. The woman on the phone said she understood my frustration, but their policy prevented her from canceling our room without me paying for the night. We had no choice but to suck it up and stay for at least one night, but knowing how hard rooms were to find at the moment, I decided we would go ahead and tough it out for our entire 2-night stay.

I was frustrated, and I was ready to give up. I was growing weary of the journey and I could not figure out how the moving was helping anyone.

We checked into the Super 8 and brought in all our things from Jackie's car. Like the hotel itself, the room was not well lit, and it smelled of cigarette smoke. Despite the smell and look of the room, it appeared to be clean. Since I was a bit of a germaphobe, I checked the beds for bed bugs, hair, or any other signs of filth, and thankfully found nothing. The bathroom seemed to be clinging to life. The tub and toilet were barely working, but they too looked clean. The sink looked as if it was ready to fall to the ground at any moment, but amazingly it still worked.

The hotel room was very basic. The only luxury was cable TV, but we were not there for the amenities. We just needed a place to sleep, and for the next two nights that would be taken care of, so we were fine.

Once all of our items were in the room, I walked to a nearby grocery store to pick up food for Malachi and me. The hotel room had a refrigerator and microwave, which meant I could buy food that could be heated. I walked around the store looking for items that were both healthy and practical. I found Malachi's favorite tea, Peace Tea. It was a treat for him, and it brought me a small measure of comfort to be able to get it for him.

It had been a long day, and we were tired, so I picked up some food that we could heat and eat quickly. When we finished dinner, I told Malachi to shower and get in the bed while I took Jackie's car back to her. I made my way to Jackie's house, and she graciously gave me a ride back to the hotel. As much as I appreciated her help, I knew it was a lot for her to help us as much as she did, and I hoped it was not too much.

When I got back to the hotel, I got in bed and went to sleep. I was tired and frustrated, but as much as I wanted to give up, I knew I couldn't because God had a plan.

The next day I got Malachi to school using Southwest Prime. It took them more than an hour to get him there, but he was at school, and I was thankful he didn't have to miss a day from school. Once he left, I waited for the Arby's across the street to open so that I could use their free Wi-Fi to look for a job and a place to stay. The hotel had free Wi-Fi, but the room was so dark – even with the lights on – that I just felt exhausted. I needed light, and I was not getting enough of it in the room.

Once I got to Arby's, I realized that they did not have electrical outlets, so I ended up back at the hotel anyway. I was frustrated that the room was not up to the standards I was used to, but I was thankful we were not on the street.

Jackie loaned me her car again that evening. Unfortunately, that meant she had to pick me up from the hotel and drive me back to her home so that I could drive the car back to the hotel. It was a process, but I was thankful she allowed me to use her car the next day to check out of the hotel and go to my interview with Best Buy.

The next day we got up early so we could check out before it was time to drop Malachi off at school. The hotel did not have a dolly, so we had to take all of our bags and suitcases to the car one by one. When we left Connecticut, we each had one suitcase and two bags containing our clothes and personal items. We also had non-perishable food that we carried with us from hotel to hotel. My suitcase was full of clothes, books, and journals, so it was heavy.

Each time we changed hotels, we had to lug all our stuff from the room to the car and then from the car to the room. I was getting weary of the process, both physically and emotionally. I was ready to get our own place and get back some resemblance of a normal life. Days were beginning to feel like weeks and weeks like months.

Once we packed up, I dropped Malachi off at school and stopped for breakfast at McDonald's. I only had a few dollars to eat with, but I needed to eat something before my interview. After I ate, I drove to Best Buy, found parking, and went in for my interview.

Best Buy's headquarters was massive, and part of the interview process was a tour of the facility. Three large buildings intersected in one circle in the middle. It was more of a campus than the building I was expecting. The Best Buy corporate campus had everything one could need throughout the workday – there were two coffee shops, a full-service restaurant, a gym, and a store. The DMV also came to the campus, and there were options for the post office. I was excited about the prospect of having access to all of that right at work.

I sat down for the interview, and it seemed that everything was going well. But I had felt confident about the first job I interviewed for as well, so I would not allow myself to get too excited until I had an official written offer. The interviewers seemed to be impressed with my background, and I thought it was a pretty good fit – everything except the hours. The job I interviewed for was a 2nd shift technical support role, and while I did not want to work the 2nd shift, I needed a job. I agreed to the hours, hoping that I could work the 2nd shift until a slot on the 1st shift opening.

The interview didn't last long, but I was sure I would get a callback. I asked the interviewers how long it would be before they reached a decision, and they told me that I should hear back from them in approximately two weeks when they completed their interviews. I needed to start work before then, but at that point, all I could do was wait and continue to apply for other positions until the powers that be at Best Buy made their decision.

After the interview at Best Buy, I drove to a nearby Starbucks because I also had a phone interview scheduled for that day. At 1 pm, I waited for the company to contact me, but after about 10 minutes of not hearing anything, I emailed the interviewer. She called soon after, and we talked about the position – technical support for a security company. If hired, my job would be to provide support for their products to their dealers, but not the public. I did not know their products, but I was confident I could learn them.

The interviewer and I had a great conversation, but I could not get a read as to whether I was doing well or not. One of the last questions she asked me was to provide her step-by-step instructions on making a peanut butter and jelly sandwich. In all my years of working in technical support, I've had many interviews, but no one had ever asked me that type of question. I answered it and laughed as I did because it seemed so illogical. My laughter seemed to break the ice a little bit, but not much. I asked her what the next step would be, and she said that they wanted me to come in for an interview. She asked if I could come in on the 23rd, which was two days away. I told her that day worked for me, and we agreed upon a time. The interviewer sent me an email confirming the face-to-face interview, and I was hopeful that this process would work a little bit faster than the one at Best Buy.

Once I was done with the interview, I packed my things, picked up Malachi from school, and headed to Jackie's house. I was not sure about the next move, but I believed God had a plan. Jackie and I talked while we drove to her bank, and she said she would give me the money for two nights at the Super 8 in Shakopee. She said she had been compensated for her work at the church, and she did not mind sharing it with me so that Malachi and I would have a place for the next couple of nights. I was immensely thankful for her and I did not expect her to pay for more nights for us, but I was thankful. I thank God for her obedience and generosity.

When Jackie and I arrived back at her house, she let me take her car and go to the hotel. Since the hotel was in Shakopee, I would need to take Malachi to and from school, so Jackie told me I could keep the car for a couple of days.

| 10 |

Flapping Our Wings

When we arrived at the Super 8 in Shakopee, I checked in using the cash that Jackie gave me. Once we checked in, we lugged our bags to our room on the 2nd floor. The hotel did not have an elevator, so we only carried our essential items to the room and left what we did not need in Jackie's car. Malachi took his suitcase, and I carried the food, my laptop, and a bag of toiletries.

There was a refrigerator, a microwave, and two double beds when we arrived in the room. But when I went into the bathroom, I noticed that both the tub and toilet were dirty. I was mortified. I had just paid good money for this room only to find the bathroom – the place where we do our most intimate business – unclean! It was disgusting.

I immediately called downstairs to tell the front desk what I found. The woman on the phone was not happy that I called, but I did not care. After waiting what seemed to be hours, the night receptionist came up to clean the bathroom. I felt bad because I'd seen him come on duty while we were checking in, but I needed to have the bathroom cleaned so Malachi could get his shower and we could both get to bed.

The receptionist worked on cleaning the bathroom for nearly an hour, and it looked like he wasn't getting anywhere. I finally told him he could leave because my son needed to shower, and we had to get up early in the morning. I knew it wasn't the receptionist's fault, but I was frustrated and disappointed with the room's quality.

While I tried to calm down, Malachi took his shower, and we went to bed. In the morning, we were up early because Malachi needed to be at school before the bell rang. He got dressed and headed downstairs to breakfast while I got dressed. We left in plenty of time to get him to school on time, and I followed my GPS so I could get Malachi to school without issue.

After dropping Malachi off, I plugged the hotel's address into the GPS to head back to the room. Getting to the school hadn't been bad, so I thought the drive back would be fine, but my GPS had other plans. I was about halfway to the hotel when I came to a traffic circle. I followed my GPS, and the next thing I knew, I was back at the traffic circle. I tried following the GPS again, and this time it took me down a back road to a street full of what looked like million-dollar estates.

I thought, "OK, Lord, what are you showing me here?" I did not want to stop because I wanted to get back to the hotel, but I felt like this was a place I needed to see, although I didn't know why. I continued driving, and again I was back at the traffic circle. I was beginning to feel like I was living out a scene from Groundhog Day, and I was getting frustrated.

As I continued to drive and listen to the GPS, I started to talk to God. I needed to get back to the hotel, but I knew that he was showing me something. I finally drove around the traffic circle and decided not to follow the GPS and take what I now recognized as the road I took when taking Malachi to school. I made it back to the hotel and I was thankful.

This GPS failure was a lesson for me. It was a lesson about trusting myself and trusting that I hear God's voice. I realized that once I talked to God, the voice of the GPS became background noise and I could see what I needed to do to get back to the hotel. It didn't mean that the GPS wasn't helpful at some point, because it was, but I needed to trust that I hear God above all else. I also needed to be reminded that systems fail, just as my GPS did that day but when systems fail, God does not. It was an interesting lesson and definitely a crazy way to learn it.

As thankful as I was to get back to the hotel, I realized that I was supposed to stop at Target to pick up a few things. While I waited for Target to open, I called and talked with my prayer partner. It had been awhile since we prayed together, and it was good to catch up. We both missed the season when we prayed together daily, but with the moves Malachi and I had to make every day, our prayer time was something I could no longer commit to the way I had previously.

I shared with her about the transitions and the provisions God made for Malachi and me. I hoped that we could take time to pray that morning, but there wasn't time and that was OK. Our lives had changed dramatically since we started our faith journeys and while we were both happy that God was moving, we were both in a new season of our lives. Our times of prayer had shifted to text messages, IM's and the occasional phone call to keep up with one another. It was different, but we still covered one another in prayer.

When I arrived back at the hotel, I ate breakfast and I planned on taking a nap. Just as I was about to lay down, my phone rang, and it was Best Buy. At the same time, my friend Jayme called to check on me, but I knew I had to call her back. As I hoped the recruiter from Best Buy was calling to offer me the position, but the salary they were offering was insufficient so I asked the recruiter if the salary could be adjusted for my experience. He said he would contact his manager and get back to me. I was excited to have a job offer finally and I was hopeful that they would agree to the salary I requested.

After speaking with the Best Buy recruiter, I called Jayme back. I told her about the offer and the job. She was excited, but she understood the salary issue. She asked me where Malachi and I were and what my plan was going forward. We had talked a few days before, and she was aware of the challenges we faced. I told her that God had moved for us and provided two nights at the Super 8 hotel. I told Jayme that Malachi and I were slated to check out of the Super 8 the next day, but I was believing God for the money for another hotel stay.

I was living every day by faith, and each time we had to move, I believed God more than I did the last time. Every time I was unsure where we would go, God sent someone to bless us with funds or a hotel stay. As I spoke to Jayme, I was not upset or anxious. I simply believed that God would move for us again. He was continually showing me that He was faithful. He had told me to move, and He would provide for me in my obedience.

While we were on the phone, Jayme asked me what hotel I wanted to stay in when I left the Super 8. I explained that the TownPlace in Eden Prairie was ideal because Malachi could get the bus to school, and we could walk to the market. She said OK, and we continued to talk about other things. At some point in the conversation, I told Jayme about Jackie using her points to help us with rooms. Jayme mentioned that she thought she had Marriott points too. I said, ok, but I didn't ask her to use them. I didn't want to interfere with what God was doing by asking for help when He hadn't told me to do so.

After a while, Jayme told me she would call me back later. A few minutes later, I received a text from Jayme that contained a photo. I looked at the picture and started to cry. The text showed a reservation Jayme had made for Malachi and me at the TownPlace in Eden Prairie. She had used her points to book us a room for three nights. I probably shouldn't have been surprised because that was the type of friend Jayme was, but I was shocked and amazed at God. He had once again miraculously provided for us.

When I picked Malachi up from school, I shared the news with him that we were going back to the TownPlace hotel, and we were both relieved. That evening, we spent time talking and watching TV together. After we had dinner, we prepared to move again. I went to sleep that night with a grateful heart. While I was ready to be in our own place, I was thankful to have provisions for a few more days.

The next day I went to the TownPlace hotel after dropping Malachi off at school in the hopes that I could get into the room early. However, the hotel did not have a room ready for us, so I had to wait. I talked with Jackie and decided to meet her later that evening at her son's game to return her car. She had let me hold her car to check into TownPlace, get Malachi to and from school, and attend my job interview for the security company. It was going to be a busy day, but I was ready for it.

| 11 |

Going Through the Flood

When I dropped Malachi off at school, I stopped by my post office box and then went to Starbucks to wait until I could check into the hotel. At Starbucks, I checked my messages, looked for a place to live, and applied for more jobs. I had one interview that went well, and I was scheduled for another one that day, but I was going to keep looking until I had a signed offer.

My interview was scheduled for 1:30 pm, so I did not stay at Starbucks long. I left and drove over to Bloomington, where I would interview with the security company. Before applying, I had never heard of the company or its products, but I was intrigued and needed a job.

I took the elevator to the floor I was to be interviewed on, signed in, and waited for my interviewer to come out to get me. While I sat there, a man came out with red sneakers on, and I thought about how progressive the company was to allow their employees to wear sneakers to work; I was impressed.

During my interview, we went over the details of the position. Everything was going well, and then they told me there was a second part of the interview that would happen that day. During part two, I would meet some of the company's managers. However, I wasn't told about a potential second interview, and I didn't have the time to talk to the managers that day.

I explained to the interviewer that I had a prior commitment, and she said that she would reschedule the second portion of my interview. She revealed that she hadn't told me about the second part of the interview because not everyone gets to that point. It turned out that the managers were swamped that day anyway, so rescheduling was best for everyone.

I left the interview thankful and drove to pick up Malachi from school. I picked him up and went to the TownPlace to check-in. This time we were in a room on the first floor with one queen bed and a pull-out sofa, but no extra room. Malachi missed the extra space, with one TV for both of us, but we were grateful to be in a hotel that was clean and safe.

Once we brought our bags in, I left to take Jackie's car to her. I met her at her son's game, and then we all rode back to her house. We talked a bit when I got to her place, and then, she gave me a ride back to the hotel. On the way back, we praised God for providing another hotel stay for Malachi and me. I didn't know what we would do on Monday, but we were secure for the moment; I would let God worry about the future.

Malachi and I stayed in the hotel on Friday and Saturday. The mall was close by, but we did not have any money, so we rested in the room. Malachi played his video game, and I surfed the web, looking for a place for us to live. I was well aware that it would be hard for me to get us a home without having a job yet, but I still looked. I knew it was just a matter of time before I either received a revised offer from Best Buy or another position. I also took the opportunity to send an email, complete with pictures, to the Wyndham Hotel corporate office regarding the horrific service we'd received at two of their Super 8 hotels.

That weekend, when I got discouraged, I prayed, and I blogged. The more I wrote, and the more I prayed, the better I felt. I was regaining myself in the middle of all the chaos. I even became bold enough to record my thoughts and feelings on video. I thought the videos would be easy, but it was hard being exposed and sharing my pain.

As hard as it was, I felt that the videos were necessary so that others would not feel alone when they found themselves in the middle of God's plan for their lives. I still had faith, but people needed to see my tears. They needed to know that I had doubts and fears. They needed to know about the instability, the frustration, the heartache, the tenacity, the fire, and the feelings of loss.

Fortunately, God didn't let us go through any of our journey alone. I had friends praying for Malachi and me during this time. Sometimes I would send my prayer partner-specific prayer requests. Other times people would call at just the right time. Others would send much-needed financial help. It was amazing how God would lay us on the hearts of people. It was good to know that even though we were the ones taking the steps on this journey, we were never alone.

Before we left Connecticut, I had prophetic dreams that gave me hints about the future. I didn't know how to interpret them at the time, so I wrote them down. One of the dreams I had in Connecticut was about Malachi and I driving my white Ford Edge down a road, and people were watching along the sides of the road like we were part of a parade.

We drove down the street through what appeared to be a puddle. The puddle grew into a large body of water, and as we drove, I could sense that the people on the street were wondering if we were going to make it through the flood. I could see the faces in the crowd, and they were all familiar to me. I kept driving, confident that we would make it through the water, and we did. For me, the water looked like a small puddle, not the flood that everyone else saw.

I continued to drive, and we were soon on a winding bridge, and off to the left, I could see ocean waves headed our way. Just as the ocean waves were about to overtake the bridge, we were suddenly in what I believe was our home by the water, safe and sound.

As I look back on the dream, I realize that God was likely showing me that Malachi and I would have witnesses to our tough season. People would be concerned, rightfully so, but we would be safe and sound in the end. God had shown me what was to come. I just had to wait for the manifestation. It was true, we were going through a tough time, but my faith was in God to carry us through. As we ended our time at TownPlace, I was unsure where we would go, but I knew God would provide for us. He always did.

Saturday evening, I spoke with one of our friends from Connecticut. I had planned on calling her, but she reached out to me instead. She asked how things were going, and I explained that we had been blessed with enough money for a hotel until Monday, but I was unsure what God would do after that. She told me she would send me money and asked for the best way to get it to me. After some discussion, we decided on a Walmart to Walmart. She did not tell me how much she was sending, but I believed it would be enough to get us another room on Monday. God was providing for us in ways that I did not expect or anticipate, so I expected that Monday would be the same thing.

On Sunday, Jackie took us to church, and I prayed for God to move as He did before. On the way back to the hotel, I got a message that I could pick up the money from Walmart. Jackie drove me to Walmart to pick up the funds, which unfortunately were not enough to cover another night at the hotel. Although I was thankful for financial help in any amount, I was at a loss as to what I was supposed to do next.

When we got back to the hotel, Jackie asked me what I would do. I didn't know what to tell her. We planned for Malachi to take the Southwest Prime to school on Monday while I packed up and moved to our next location. But now, I did not know where that location would be. All I knew to do was pray, trust, and believe God. He had done it before, so I knew He would do it again.

| 12 |

Moments of Rest

We checked out of TownPlace with no idea where we would go. We had a bit of money from my generous friend, but we would need to add to it to get a room for a couple of nights. We didn't know where the extra money would come from, but we trusted God. When the time came to check out, I was not as afraid as I had been other times, but I was still nervous.

By the time Jackie came to get me, I had received more funds from another friend, but I was unsure if it was enough to get a room. We left the hotel, picked up Malachi from school, and headed back to Jackie's house. We figured out that the Motel 6 had rooms available, and I had enough to cover two nights. I felt a lot better once I knew where we were going.

Jackie allowed me to use her car to check into the motel and take Malachi to school the next day. As we were leaving, Jackie told me about a deal for food at LeeAnn Chin's restaurant. With the deal, Malachi and I could both eat dinner for under $10. I was thankful that God had provided not only our room but also our food for the night.

When we arrived at the motel to check-in, the clerk asked if we preferred a particular floor. I chose the first floor because I assumed staying on the first floor would mean we wouldn't have to drag our luggage up steps, but I was wrong. In reality, the first floor was the basement.

There were no guest rooms on the same floor as the hotel office. So, we took our items out of Jackie's car and dragged them down the stairs to our room. Once we got settled, we sat down to watch the presidential debate.

The next day after I took Malachi to school, I drove Jackie's car back to her house, and she dropped me back off at the motel. On the way back to the motel, we discussed God, family, and faith. I had my second interview for the security company that day, and we were both excited about it. Jackie told me she would pick Malachi up from school and drop him back off at the motel for me, so I could focus on being present with the managers of the company.

I arrived for my second interview, excited yet pensive. I was anxious to get a decent job, so we could finally get a place and stop hotel hopping. I was thankful for the opportunity to come back for the second part of the interview, and I was hopeful that an official employment offer would soon follow.

When I entered the conference room on the 24th floor, I noticed the beautiful view of Minneapolis and the surrounding cities. Shortly after I arrived, three interviewers entered the conference room, and we had a great conversation. It was the best interview I had ever been a part of, and I knew I had the job. Before I left, the managers asked me to either tell them a joke or give them my best Batman impersonation. I could not think of a joke, so I gave them the best Batman impression I could muster, and we all got a great laugh out of it.

I headed back to the hotel in a Lyft, and by the time I arrived, Malachi was in the room. We talked about his day first, and then I shared the highlights of my interview. I asked him if he was embarrassed that I made the Batman impression, and he said no; he was actually impressed. I could tell the thought of me impersonating Batman was hilarious to him.

The rest of the evening was a rare respite from the chaos. Malachi and I continued chatting as we ordered and ate pizza. The next day we would check out and again move to some unknown destination. The next day would be riddled with uncertainty, but that evening we relaxed. We had no choice but to trust God as we had done every day since leaving Connecticut. The next morning, we would have to trust Him for provision, but we indulged in His rest that night.

| 13 |

Hitting the Rocks

The next morning, we checked out of the Motel 6, and I took the familiar drive to Malachi's school using Jackie's car. By now, we were used to hectic mornings. Unfortunately, we were also used to uncertain evenings. Malachi didn't ask me where we would be going when I picked him up that afternoon, but I knew that he was worried.

I know our journey looked insane to people who didn't believe like me, but I knew we were supposed to be in Minnesota. I was a single mom, and it was hard for me to watch my son worry about not having a consistent roof over his head, but I knew life would be great as soon as we got settled.

After I dropped Malachi at school, I tried to figure out where we would go that night. I went to Starbucks and got one cup of coffee with the money I had on me. I had Jackie's car, but I didn't want to drive if I didn't have to. I still had not found a place to stay by the time Malachi got out of school. Not knowing what else to do, I retrieved my son, and we headed to church for Bible Study.

Jackie and I had talked throughout the day, so she knew I did not have a place to go that night. We were both praying fervently. I was beginning to feel bad about having to depend on her so much, but I was also thankful to have someone standing in faith with me who was willing to help.

After Bible study, one of the sisters asked me about my situation and then told me that she worked for the county assisting people with housing. She gave me information on shelters and informed me that we could get housing much quicker if Malachi and I could get into a shelter. I was thankful for the information, but I did not want to use it because I was afraid of being separated from Malachi. He was 18 and I assumed he would have to go to a men's shelter. He was not built for that, and I could not even begin to think of the things he might see there.

The lady from Bible study assured me that while a shelter is not a long-term solution, it would not be as bad as I thought. I thanked her for her input, and we all left. I sincerely thought about what she said, but I still couldn't believe that God had sent us to Minnesota and provided hotel rooms every night only to have us go into a shelter. That didn't resonate with me. I was believing Him for bigger.

We drove back to Jackie's house and tried to figure out what we were going to do. Jackie looked at hotels and I was just sullen; I literally had no more strength to do this anymore and I just wanted a place. I contacted my prayer partner and asked her to pray because we needed a place to stay. It was getting late, and Malachi had to be at school in the morning. While I'm sure Jackie would've let us stay at her house, it was not an option. After talking to my prayer partner, she said she would send me $50. I added that to $20 I had received from another lady at Bible study, and I had just enough for a night at a nearby motel called The Key Inn.

My prayer partner sent the money via PayPal. I transferred the money to Jackie and gave her the $20 cash I had, so she could use her card to get our room. The motel needed Jackie to be present to use her card, so she drove us to the hotel and got us the room. Once I got Malachi situated in the room, Jackie and I went back to her house so I could borrow her car to get Malachi to school the next day. By the time I got back to the Key Inn, it was after midnight, and we needed to be up and out by 6:30 am. I was beyond tired, and not just from the events of the day. I was emotionally drained from all the searching and moving. I was ready for it all to end.

The Key Inn was another disappointment. The hallways smelled like stale cigarettes, urine, and floral air fresheners. The room was filthy as well, but by the time I got back from dropping Jackie off, Malachi was already asleep. I tried looking in his bed to see if there were bed bugs or dirty sheets, but I didn't have the heart to wake him up.

I prayed as I searched my bed. While I was thankful that God had worked it out for us to afford this room, I was appalled at the state of it. But there was no place else for us to go, so I kept reminding myself that it was only for one night. I cried, put on my pajamas, and got in bed, praying that if there were any bugs present in the room, they would not find their way into our luggage.

Admittedly, I did not sleep well that night. I tossed and turned and finally fell asleep sometime in the middle of the night. I was so tired of moving around; I just wanted to be stable. I knew God had a plan, but the process had started to get the best of me, Malachi, and even sweet Jackie. We needed a miracle just for the strength to keep moving forward.

| 14 |

Regaining Flight

We walked out of the Key Inn the next day in the same dilemma we had been in previously. We had no clue where we would lay our heads that night. The weight of the uncertainty in our lives made the days seem much longer than their usual 24 hours. I was growing weary of the movement, the uncertainty, the journey and I just wanted to get settled. I knew that God was teaching me to rely on Him in this season, but the lessons seemed to get more challenging. I wanted the lessons to be easy, but I realized that nothing worth having ever comes easy and I wanted what God had for us at the end of this journey so I would endure to the end no matter how much it hurt.

As I drove Malachi to school from the hotel, I received a call from my cousin, Ed. Ed was one of the few people on my mother's side of the family who knew I was in Minnesota. I spoke with him the day we left Connecticut, and while he was concerned about us moving, he understood my faith walk. Ed asked me how things were going, and I explained to him that God was providing daily, and I was trusting Him for a place to sleep that night.

I didn't ask my cousin for money, but he said he would send me $300 to help us with a hotel and food. I was thankful because I knew the money would be enough to get us a room for at least a few nights. Tears welled up in my eyes as I realized God had sent someone at the perfect time to help us once again. I sent Ed my PayPal link, and before the afternoon, the $300 he promised was in my account.

After I dropped Malachi off at school, I decided to head to Caribou to search for a job and a hotel room. While I was at Caribou, I spoke to my prayer partner. As we talked, I told her about the blessing I received from my cousin, and she told me that the Lord had instructed her to sow her car payment into my life. We were both shocked at God's leading because one of the things we prayed about during our prayer season while I was in Connecticut was for her to get a car. I was thrilled when the Lord answered our request. We had prayed and believed, and the Lord had provided faithfully. When she said the Lord told her to sow her car payment into my life, I was shocked, amazed, and grateful. I knew that if God told her to sacrifice her car payment, He would provide for her in another way, and He did just that.

Once we got over our initial shock, I explained that I needed to find Malachi and me a hotel room that would maximize the money I'd received because the Ryder's Cup was in full swing, and most hotels I looked at were either booked solid or priced much higher than usual. Even the Super 8 in Shakopee, which was horrendous, was charging more than $400 a night for the weekend; it was crazy! As my prayer partner and I talked, she told me about a website that might help me get a deal on a hotel. She looked on her deal website as I looked on hotel websites. I was trying my best to get something close to Malachi's school so that I could get him to class on time. I actually hoped to go back to the TownPlace in Eden Prairie because the mall was close by, and Malachi could take the SouthWest Prime to and from school.

Unfortunately, the TownPlace had no availability, so I checked surrounding hotels, and they were either all booked or too expensive. We continued to talk and look for hotels, and at almost the same time, we both saw that the Hampton Inn in Maple Grove had rooms available for a reasonable rate. I booked the room immediately. Finally, Malachi and I were set for the weekend, and again, I was thankful we had someplace to go.

While I was waiting for Malachi to finish school, I went by to see an apartment that I found online. I was desperately hoping my credit wouldn't be an issue. When I arrived at the complex, I realized that it was further back than I anticipated, and I wondered how we would get around because I didn't have a car. I decided to go in anyway, believing that God would work it out.

The complex had an on-site fitness center and recreation room, along with several other fantastic amenities. The apartments themselves were beautiful with garages and gas stoves. I loved everything about the apartment, so I really hoped I could get a unit.

The manager showed me around and asked me when I wanted to move in, so I told him as soon as possible. They had an apartment available, so he told me to complete the application. Since there was an application fee, I decided to ask about the chances of getting the apartment, given that I was evicted from my last place, and my credit was not good. The manager let me know that my application would not be approved, but I should call him and try again if something changed. I left disappointed but willing to see what God would do next. After all, I knew that God would not send us all the way to Minnesota, only to have me turn around and go back home.

I drove back to Eden Prairie to wait for Malachi to finish school, and I continued to look online for other apartments that might give us a chance. I had one job offer from Best Buy, and I was confident the salary would be enough to get us a place when they called back with the pay increase. And I was anticipating a job offer from Alarm.com, which would also be enough to get us a place to stay. The finances were on the horizon. I just needed to find a landlord willing to give us a chance.

After I picked up Malachi from school, we headed over to the Hampton Inn and checked in. Once there, Malachi did his homework, and I checked my email. After Malachi finished his assignments, we drove to get dinner. A nearby shopping center had good options for both of us. We settled on LeeAnn Chin because Malachi enjoyed their food the first time we went, and they had great vegetarian options, which were difficult to find at most places. With our dinner in hand, we headed back to the hotel. Along the way, we talked, laughed, and joked with one another.

God is so awesome. It's just like Him to show up in the middle of a mess and restore the relationship between a mother and son. See, God's focus is always people. We are often distracted, wanting God to get us out of troubling situations. But God is more concerned with the trouble brewing within us and how that trouble is affecting the people we love. While this season, in the middle of my faith journey, was stressful, I would endure it for the rest of my life if it meant my son would continue to laugh with me while learning to trust God.

The next day I took Malachi to school and headed back to Caribou to wait to look for an apartment online. I did not want to drive around, wasting gas for things that would not pan out. I knew I needed to replace the gas I used, and I had to be wise with spending because I hadn't started a job yet.

As I waited for Malachi's school day to end, I finally called some of my family members to tell them we were in Minnesota. Before we left Connecticut, I decided that I could only tell those I knew would have faith to believe with me, and unfortunately, that did not include many of my family members. I knew if I had talked to anyone without the level of faith I had, they would try to talk me out of it.

My Aunt Kneata, my dad's sister, was my first call, and as I expected, she was shocked that I up and moved Malachi and me across the country. However, she did reveal that we had a cousin who also lived in Minnesota. I was shocked. Aunt Kneata explained who he was and how we were related, then she told me she would connect me to him on Facebook. I was excited because I thought he might have a home large enough to take Malachi and me in until I could get us a place. I did not know where my cousin lived, but I hoped he was in a position to help us until I got on my feet.

I waited impatiently for the friend request. I knew my Aunt Kneata would connect us, but then I would have to wait on him to respond. I was hoping the whole process would go quickly.

In the meantime, I continued searching online for apartments. I knew I had a good chance of getting both the job at Best Buy and the job at Alarm.com, so I kept searching for a home for Malachi and me. I also worked on promotions for my books, journals, and other entrepreneurial services to earn money while we waited on a steady paycheck.

Before leaving Connecticut, I began working with a couple of clients on graphic design and website projects, so during our transition, I continued working for these clients during the day. It wasn't easy to get new clients because we were always on the move, but I used coffee shops and the public library as my office. Thankfully, whenever I needed extra money, a new project would come in. Those funds were usually not enough to pay for a night in a hotel, so I used them to cover my cell phone bill and other necessities. My business projects also kept me busy during the day when I got frustrated with job and apartment hunting.

When it was time to get to Malachi, I gathered my things so we could stop at the grocery store and pick up some food before heading to the hotel. It was a Friday, and Jackie let me know she would need her car for the weekend, so I had to make sure we were prepared to stay at the hotel for the rest of the weekend. When I booked the hotel, I made sure the room had a refrigerator and a microwave so we could store and heat food.

Just as we were settling into the hotel room, I received a phone call from a number I did not recognize. I thought it was another interview request or a job offer, but it was a senior customer care representative from Wyndham hotels. She told me she had received my email from the CEO and wanted the opportunity to make things right. She expressed her sorrow for our experiences and offered me two free nights at any Wyndham hotel.

Knowing our situation, I requested three nights, but she could only provide me with two. Of course, I accepted. She told me that the points would be credited to my account immediately, and I breathed a sigh of relief. God had taken care of us for two more days.

This whole process was a day-by-day lesson in faith. Each day, I learned to trust God more. Each day I had to pick up my resolve from the day before and increase it. Some days, God showed up at the last second, and those were the scariest times. But He never left us. I thought this daily faith walk must've been what the Israelites experienced in the wilderness – literally following God wherever He led. It was difficult, and often I felt crazy, but I knew we needed to be in Minnesota.

I could not relay to people how I knew I needed to be in Minnesota, but this was not just an ordinary move for me. It was a life-or-death scenario, and I had to allow God a chance to make it work on my behalf. As difficult as it was not knowing where we would stay every day, I knew that there was no going back to Connecticut or New Jersey.

Not long after I received the call from Wyndham, I received a call from the security company officially offering me a position. That same day, I also received a call from Best Buy with an updated salary offer. God was showing out. The revised salary offer from Best Buy was about the same as the security company's offer, so now I had to make a decision. Both companies were great, and I looked forward to working at either one, but I had to make the best decision for Malachi and me.

The offer at Best Buy was for a position starting October 17th, working from 3:30 pm to12 am on Sunday thru Thursday. The job at the security company was for daytime hours and began on October 31st. In addition to the work hours, I also had to consider location. I didn't have a car, so I only wanted to accept a job I would be able to get to and from using public transportation. I preferred the Best Buy position, but I agreed to both opportunities. I decided that I would find a place to live first, and that would help me determine what position to make permanent. When I told Jackie about the two offers, she was happy for me, but she agreed that the evening position could be problematic.

Later that evening, I used my Wyndham account points to book us a room at the Super 8 in Bloomington. The reviews were much better than the previous Super 8's we stayed at, and I knew the area because it was right behind the LaQuinta we stayed at when we first arrived in Minnesota. I booked our room for two nights starting on Sunday.

On Sunday, Malachi and I checked out of the Hampton Inn and went to church with a couple who lived close by the hotel. They agreed to pick us up, take us to church, and drop us off at the Super 8 hotel once service was over.

| 15 |

A Moment of New

On the way back to the hotel, the couple giving us a ride asked if we'd ever been to the Mall of America. I said that we had not because of all the moving, and they suggested that we go. The way they described it made it sound wonderful, but I did not want to go without money. Our friends assured us that we could go and spend very little. So, Malachi and I decided that we would go that afternoon. The Super 8 had a free shuttle to Mall of America, so we hopped on it as soon as we got settled.

We had heard of the Mall of America, but neither of us knew what to expect. When we walked in, we were in awe. The Mall of America is an experience all on its own. I understood why people flew from all over the world to shop there. When we walked in, we stood there wide-eyed like kids in a huge candy store. The mall was massive, and there was a full amusement park in the center. As we walked around the mall, I saw almost every store I could think of and even some I had never imagined. Malachi said that every other mall was simply a shopping center compared to the Mall of America. We spent a couple of hours walking around and there was still so much more left to see, but it was getting late and I had to get Malachi to school in the morning. We found one of the food courts (there are several), we had dinner, and headed back to the hotel.

The next day, I did not have Jackie's car to get Malachi to school, so I had to get him there on the bus. I figured out that we could get from Bloomington, where the Super 8 was, to Eden Prairie, where he could take the SouthWest Prime to school. The only issue was we had to leave by 6 am to get the first bus, which meant we had to be up at 4:15 am to take our showers and get dressed. I tried to make sure we did everything we could the night before, so we would have very little to do in the morning. I hated that we had to get up so early, but I was determined to make sure my son received his education.

Waking my son up before dark to shuffle him on three buses to get him to school made me feel like a horrible parent. I often questioned the Lord because this was not what I envisioned for us at all. It was not my plan to be transient, especially with Malachi in his senior year of high school. It was the worst time of my life as a parent. I felt like I had taken my son into a sea of the unknown. I could've withstood the waves myself, but watching him wake up with fear threatening to overtake him, was almost my undoing.

I believed that it would all work out for our good, but I understood what Malachi felt because I felt it too – the disappointment, the anxiety, the fear, the doubt, and the nervousness of being without a stable home in a state where we had no family. It was difficult for me to look at him at times because I knew he was hurting, but I was doing everything I could to change our situation, and I knew once I got a job and we were able to get a place, things would begin to get back to normal.

I didn't know what else to do, so I turned to God. I knew He had a plan, but in the middle of the madness, it seemed like uncertainty was everywhere. I wondered if I had made the right choice - if I had actually heard God right. We were beyond tired, and I was almost ready to throw in the towel. In my feeble human mind, I could not conceive that what I was going through was in God's plans.

I felt like I had to have heard wrong, but in my heart, I knew that wasn't the case. I knew we were supposed to be in Minnesota; I just could not figure out why we had to lose so much to get here. I spent many nights crying because I just did not understand why this was the way it needed to happen.

After Malachi boarded the Southwest Prime to school, I walked over to the nearby Caribou Coffee. I did not have access to a vehicle, so I took the opportunity to sit in Caribou and work on client projects and my websites while Malachi was in school. When he got out, the Southwest Prime bus brought him back to the transit station, and we took two buses back to the hotel. Once we were back at the hotel, we had just enough time to go to the gas station to get something to eat for dinner.

Each night was a different type of fast food. I wondered how people could eat healthy in situations like ours. Most of our dinners had to be prepared in a microwave or delivered. I loved eating out as much as the next person, but, like everything else, it was beginning to wear on me.

Before moving to Minnesota, I lost 50 pounds by changing some of my eating habits, but with all the eating out we were doing, those pounds were starting to creep back on me. I tried to make good choices whenever I could, but there were times when eating well was just not within the budget.

The next day we were back up before dawn to catch the bus, but instead of waiting for Malachi to finish school, I had to make my way back to the hotel to meet Jackie. We had to check out of the Super 8, and once again, I had no idea where we were going to sleep that night.

Jackie met me at the hotel, we loaded up her car, and she asked me where I wanted to go. I asked her to take me back out to Eden Prairie, so I could wait for Malachi to finish school. I was praying that by the time school was out, I would have the money for another hotel room. Jackie dropped me off at the Starbucks near the mall in Eden Prairie and said she would check in with me later to see where to bring my things. I knew this was taking a toll on both of us, but I was thankful for her help.

I walked into Starbucks and got coffee and ice water, which was about all I had the money for at the moment. I worked on my computer and believed God for a move. At some point, my Aunt Lorna called me to find out how we were doing. I responded that we were in Minnesota, and she was shocked. She asked me how it was going, and I told her that God was providing for us day-by-day; we were just waiting for him to provide for that night.

My Aunt Lorna had helped us in the past when we lived with my friend in Connecticut. She would order groceries for us online and have them sent to the house. I knew she was generous, but I did not expect her to help us get a room. She asked me if there was a place we could go, and I told her about a deal I found for a week's stay at the Chanhassen Inn for $400. She told me she would loan me $400. I did not expect or anticipate this, but once again, God showed himself strong.

When I hung up with Aunt Lorna, I called the Chanhassen Inn, only to find out that the weeklong rooms were all sold out. I was once again disappointed, but I didn't have time to cry. I had to find somewhere safe for my son and me to stay. The Ryder's cup was over, but I did not think we could get another room for a week for under $400. I had to fight to believe we would get what we needed.

I spoke to Jackie, and I told her that my aunt had provided funds for us, but the Chanhassen Inn was booked. I told her I was looking for another place that had availability. I wanted to try the TownePlace again because I really liked staying there, and it was close enough to school that Malachi could get the SouthWest Prime to class. However, when we walked over to ask about accommodations, they had no rooms either.

I checked my PayPal balance as I waited for Jackie to pick us up and take us to our next destination – wherever that would be. I was startled to see a charge I hadn't authorized that took almost half the money Aunt Lorna sent to me. I was furious! It turned out that even if the TownPlace had rooms available, I would not have had enough money to book one because the charge was nearly $200. I needed to figure out what this charge was for, but I knew I wouldn't get anywhere with PayPal after business hours.

When Jackie arrived to get us, I asked her to take us to Motel 6 because the listing online said the rooms were less than $60 a night. I planned to book a room for one night and then find somewhere else to stay once PayPal issued my refund. Since this was our 2nd stay at the Motel 6, Jackie knew I would need her car to get Malachi to school and check out of the hotel the following day. Once we got settled in the room, I drove Jackie back home then headed back to Motel 6. As we had done previously, Malachi and I just took what we needed and left the bulk of our things in Jackie's car.

The next morning, I got us both up, and we got dressed so that Malachi could get to school. We also checked out of Motel 6 because I was hopeful that I could get the issue resolved and get into a different hotel. Unlike the Hampton Inn and Super 8, Motel 6 did not offer free breakfast, refrigerators, and microwaves, but honestly, I was just thankful for a safe place to sleep. Malachi qualified for free breakfast and lunch at school, so I advised him to eat breakfast and lunch there, and I would figure something out for myself.

Since I had Jackie's car, I decided to apply for assistance in Minnesota. I'd been using our Connecticut benefits, but every time I used the card I was afraid some big burly man was going to arrest me for fraud. I also knew that the only way we could get housing help in Minnesota was to be on assistance in Minnesota.

There was an office close to Motel 6, so I drove there after dropping Malachi off at school. I applied for the benefits and was approved for the services to start the next month. Thankfully, they also provided me with a list of housing agencies. I hoped our next home was on this list. I also used their food shelf to get non-perishable food just in case we end up back at Motel 6 that night.

When I picked Malachi up from school, he asked me if he could go to the library, and I told him we could. He wanted to check out a book, but the library wanted proof of address, and unfortunately, we did not have that. So, I drove to our post office to check our mail, hoping that any stamped correspondence would be sufficient for him to get a library card. I was glad that I checked my mail because there was a notice that we would stop receiving Connecticut benefits on October 31st, so I had applied for Minnesota benefits just in time.

We headed back to the library, and while Malachi did his homework, I called about the charge on my PayPal account. It turned out that it was an accurate charge for something I thought was free. I tried to explain my situation to the person on the other end of the phone, but they said that the charge would remain. I was devastated because that money could have sustained us a few more days. Refusing to give in to despair, I decided to take our remaining money and book a room at the Super 8. At least at that hotel, we would be near the bus, I could get Malachi to school on my own, and we would have a microwave and refrigerator in our room.

When we got ready to leave the library, Malachi still wanted to check out some books, and the librarian allowed him to, even though we did not have a physical address in Eden Prairie. Interestingly enough, until that time in our lives, I took for granted how many things you need a physical address for – getting books from the library, getting a job, and going to school, for example. Through my struggles, I began to understand how challenging it must be for homeless people.

We left the library and headed to Super 8 to check-in, thankfully everything went smoothly at the hotel. We had enough time to get settled and head to church for Bible study. I put the church's name into my phone's GPS, but I ended up someplace else – a church, but not our church. I tried again, and this time we ended up in St. Paul. I could not remember the church's address, and by this time, I was tired of driving, so we stopped at Walmart and headed back to the hotel. I sent Jackie a text and explained what happened. I laughed about it later; obviously, God had other plans for us that night.

We had two nights at the Super 8, and after that, I didn't know what we would do, but I was determined to trust God. The next day I drove Malachi to school and headed back to the hotel. I did not have money to sit in Starbucks all day, and quite honestly, I was tired. While I was at the hotel, I spoke to my sister-friend, Kindra, who was on her own faith journey. I updated her on our life's latest events and told her that God was providing for us daily. Kindra was one of the people in my circle whose faith matched mine, and I could be transparent with her.

It was refreshing to talk to a like-minded person. We cried and prayed together as sisters. She was believing God for me, and I was believing God for her.

After I picked up Malachi from school, we went back to the library so he could get another book then we drove to the hotel so he could start his homework. After he completed his assignments, we went to the supermarket to get dinner and headed back to the hotel. We had to check out of the hotel the next morning, and somehow I also needed to get Malachi to school and return Jackie's car. I decided that I would drop Malachi off at school, then head back to the hotel and pack up.

| 16 |

Windshears and Freefalls

After I dropped Malachi at school, I went back to the Super 8 as planned and packed up our stuff. Then I went to Jackie's house to return her car. She drove me back to Starbucks, and I waited there for Malachi to get out of school. I still had no idea where we would sleep that night, and I had no more money.

While at Starbucks, my Aunt Linda reached out to me because most of my family now knew we were in Minnesota. She asked me if we needed anything, and I told her I was believing God for a place for the night. She sent me $50 via PayPal, and while it was not enough to get a room for the night, it was more than what I had before, and I was thankful.

When Malachi texted me that school was out, I told him to take a Lyft to the Starbucks. When he arrived, we walked over to the mall because I needed to go to Target. I asked Jackie to meet us there, and she agreed. While we were there, I called Pastor Carey because I needed him to pray for me. I had no idea where we were going to go that night, and I was afraid.

Pastor Carey's wife, Pastor Nadine, answered when I called, and she said the church would help us get a room. She asked me where we were and agreed to meet us at a motel. Jackie picked us up from the mall, and we looked at places on our phones and found an inexpensive option. I called the Pastor's wife and told her about the motel we found.

When we arrived at the motel, it was not someplace I wanted to stay and not someplace that any of us felt comfortable at, so we took our bags from Jackie's car to Pastor Nadine's car, and she drove us to the Super 8 in Brooklyn Park. They had rooms available, and she negotiated three nights for us.

The Super 8 in Brooklyn Park was not as nice as the one in Bloomington, but it was not as bad as Shakopee or Chaska. The clientele was interesting, to say the least, and the smoke smell was evident, but we were able to sleep in clean beds. The only downside was that I could not get a bus to get Malachi to school. I was told to call the school and arrange a ride for him, but I was unsure how long we would be there. The school needed a lead time of at least two days to set up transportation, and since I did not know how long we would be there, I didn't call, and Malachi missed the next few days of school.

While we were at Super 8 in Brooklyn Park, I finally connected with my Cousin Royce on Facebook. We chatted over Facebook messenger, and he agreed to come and meet us in Brooklyn Park. I was happy to have family close by, and while I was not sure how things would turn out, I believed God for the best.

Royce met us at Denny's near the hotel and paid for our dinner. I knew he was related to me as soon as I saw him because he looked like my grandfather and my father. Most of the men on my dad's side of the family have a similar facial structure, and Cousin Royce definitely had it. We talked about how we were related, and I updated him on family news. He asked me how long we had been in Minnesota and why we had moved. I told him what I had been telling everyone else: I was in Minnesota because God told me to move.

I knew that sounded crazy, but it was the truth. I would not have given Minnesota a second thought if God didn't make it crystal clear that we needed to be there. Cousin Royce asked me how long we had left in the Super 8 and what we would do afterward. I told him we were there until Monday, but I did not know what I was going to do after that.

As others had, he suggested that we go into a shelter, but that was not something I wanted to do because I feared Malachi and I would be separated. He told me to let him know if things did not work out on Monday, and he would see what he could do.

Monday came, and I did not have any other options, so I called Royce. Just as he said he would, he paid for another night for us. He told me he did not have room at his place, but if things still were not looking good the next day, he would take us to the shelter. I hoped and prayed it would not come to that, but I believed God would move for us quickly if it did.

| 17 |

Shelter Day: Refusing to Give Up

We woke up Tuesday morning knowing that we needed to check out by 11. I was anxious because there was nothing left and I could not see a way forward. Royce agreed to come and take us to the shelter and if I'm honest, I was devastated. I could not believe it was about to come to this – us staying in a shelter. God had provided every single day since we arrived and I could not fathom that all of a sudden He was done providing.

When Royce arrived, we packed up his truck, and he took us to the Sharing and Caring Hands shelter in Minneapolis. As upset as I was about the situation, I had no more options and no more words. I silently prayed as we reached the front door.

We waited in line for what seemed like hours, and every minute, I was hoping that God would make another way. After waiting in line for quite some time, we went to speak to the intake worker. She asked me what we were there for, and I told her we needed shelter. She told me they would not provide shelter for Malachi and me because their shelter only provided for families of three or more. She said that while she could not provide shelter, she could give us bus tokens. While it was not a place to stay, I was thankful for the tokens so that I could get Malachi to and from school.

While I had no idea what we were going to do next, I was relieved that Malachi and I would not be separated. We did need a place to stay, but I knew that God had not provided for us every night since our arrival on August 31st, just for us to end up in a shelter. That didn't make sense to me.

Now, I believe that shelters are necessary, and they provide refuge for those who need them. I just didn't believe that was God's storyline for me. I know that may seem pompous and high-minded, but I just knew God was doing something different for us. If He had told me to go to a shelter, I would've gone, no questions asked. But He never said that to me.

As Malachi and I left Sharing and Caring Hands, the Lord spoke to me. He said that I needed to visit the shelter to see, know, and understand the plight of those I'm assigned to help. I was awestruck at the reminder that my journey was not all about me.

Royce had waited outside just in case things didn't work out at the shelter. When I told him we were denied entry, he said he would put us up for a week at the Intown Suites, but that would be all he could do for us. I was grateful for any amount of help, and I was especially thankful because, in a week, I would be a lot closer to starting my job at Best Buy.

We left the shelter, and Royce took us to his house, where we stayed until it was time for us to check into the Intown Suites.

| 18 |

Breathing Room

I was expecting the Intown Suites to be like the other hotels we had been to, but it was definitely not. Royce had mentioned that people lived there for months or years at a time, but it was a budget hotel in the strictest sense of the word. When we walked inside, there was an office to the right and a large area directly in front of us, but there was no seating or lobby like other hotels.

Royce led the way into the hotel office because he knew the manager and a few employees. He had called ahead to ensure there was availability, and thankfully we had no problem securing a room. The suite that Royce got for us had one bed and a sleeper sofa. While Malachi and I both would have preferred two beds, we were thankful to have a place to sleep.

Our room had a small kitchenette with a ¾ refrigerator, stovetop, and microwave but no oven. There was also a small dining table where we could have our meals and Malachi could do his homework. The room was small but clean. We had no complaints; it was enough for our needs.

There was a bus stop right outside the front door so I thought we would be able to get wherever we needed to go including getting Malachi to school. About a half-mile up the road, there was a supermarket, two strip malls, and a shopping mall, so while we were further out than I wanted, we were still in a good location. I was thankful that we had a place to sleep for the next seven days; a respite from all of the moving.

When we checked in, the Intown Suites provided us with a roll of toilet paper, two towels, and two washcloths. Unlike other hotels, we were responsible for washing the towels and supplying our own toilet paper. We were also responsible for anything we needed for meals: plates, pots, or utensils. And although they provided WiFi, it was not free as we had to pay a weekly fee. There was a stark difference between this hotel and others we had frequented, but Malachi and I were grateful.

After we checked in, Royce took us to the grocery store to get food, and he promised to bring us some cookware and utensils so I could cook. We were set for the week; I just needed to get Malachi back in school. It was too late to call the school when we checked in, but it was on my to-do list for the next day.

Once we settled into our room, I contacted Jackie and my prayer partner to let them both know how God had provided for us again. They supported me in prayer, and I wanted to keep them informed. They were both thrilled, and we all praised God for His faithfulness.

After talking with them, I started checking out bus schedules to see how we could get around. I was supposed to start at Best Buy in a few days, and I needed to find a transportation solution. I searched every way I could think of, but there was no way for me to get back to the Intown Suites after midnight when my shift at Best Buy ended. I could successfully get to Best Buy for the start of my shift at 3 pm, but the earliest I could get a bus back to the hotel was 4 am. That early morning bus would put me back at the hotel at 7 am, only for me to have to leave by noon to make it back to work by three. I didn't think I could sustain that kind of running around for long.

The next day Malachi and I overslept. The weight of the journey was taking a toll, and our bodies just needed rest. When Royce brought us to the Intown Suites, I noticed a Target close by, so while Malachi slept, I went to the store to pick up a few things. I left Malachi in the room because we had a limited number of bus tokens, and I knew I needed to hold onto them for another day.

When I arrived back in the room, I called Malachi's school to see if the bus could start picking him as soon as possible. He hadn't missed many classes even with our moving around, and I was trying my best to keep it that way. I knew that we had at least a week at the Intown Suites, and I was hoping we would stay longer than that. So, getting Malachi back to school was a priority. The school told me the bus would start to pick him up on Tuesday. I was grateful, but it was only Wednesday, so there were still three school days left for me to figure out.

I started looking at bus routes again, and I quickly realized that the tokens I had would not be enough to get him to school and back, even for one day. We could get the local bus, but I would need to pay for the SouthWest Prime to get him from the bus station, and I just did not have the money. Unfortunately, Malachi had to miss three more days of school while we waited on our stop to be added to the school's route.

I emailed his counselor to inform the school of our situation. I asked his teachers to send his assignments electronically. By this time, the school was aware of our circumstances, and as much as it embarrassed me, the school was very helpful.

Our first weekend at the Intown Suites, I was blessed with money that allowed me to get Malachi to school. On Monday morning, we left the Intown Suites early because his school was so far from the hotel. Once I got him to school, I decided to sit at Caribou Coffee shop next to the bus station where he took the SouthWest Prime bus until the school day concluded. When he returned to the bus station, we headed back to the hotel.

We had to take four buses to get back to the hotel, so I decided to stop at Walmart along the way to pick up some items we needed. While we were there, the rain began to come down like a monsoon, and it looked like it was not going to let up. I sighed; we still had to take two buses and then walk to the hotel. I knew I had to do something because that was a long trek to attempt without umbrellas. We would have been drenched.

While we were standing in the Walmart entryway, God reminded me of a teaching I heard from my prayer mentor, Zari Banks. She talked about having enough faith to make the rain stop. When I first heard it, I thought it was an incredible concept I hadn't thought of before. I knew that was the moment to give it a try, so I told Malachi to stay put while I went to the bathroom. I went into a stall and began to pray and speak to the rain. I commanded the rains to cease until we arrived back at the hotel.

I walked back to the entryway, but I could still hear the rain, so I continued to pray in my heavenly language under my breath. We had just a few minutes before the next bus would leave from the Mall of America to the hotel, and we still had to get from Walmart to the Mall of America. It didn't look like we would catch both buses, so I decided to order a Lyft. As the driver arrived, the rain started to slow down, and by the time we arrived at the Mall of America, it had stopped entirely. We arrived at the hotel under clear skies. I was amazed by God, and at that moment, my faith skyrocketed.

The next day the bus picked Malachi up from the hotel, and I stayed in the room. I was supposed to start my job at Best Buy, but after searching and searching, I just could not figure out how to get from Best Buy back to the Intown Suites at midnight without paying a ridiculous price for an Uber or Lyft. I had no choice but to decline the job on the day I was supposed to start working. I felt horrible about it, but I prayed and tried everything I could think of to make it work, and it just didn't. I was thankful I had also accepted the offer from the security company.

After declining Best Buy's offer, I spent time praying for the funds for another week at the Intown Suites. We only had a few days left in the week that Cousin Royce had purchased for us, but I really wanted to stay at Intown Suites since we had finally found a way for Malachi to get to school consistently.

A couple of days before our reservation ended, I had a conversation with my cousin Sam. Sam and I were pretty close, but like the rest of my family, he did not know we were in Minnesota until after we left. We finally had the chance to talk, and I was excited to share our journey with him. I told him that I was nervous, but my faith was in God to provide us with another week at the hotel. By the end of the conversation, he told me he would see if he could loan me the money for another week, and the next day, I had the money to extend our stay. I was so thankful that God gave us another week in the hotel and that I was another week closer to starting my new job. I knew that once I started the job, I would finally be able to provide a home for us in our new city.

The next day while Malachi was at school, I paid for an additional week in the room. I also searched for a place for us and completed my new hire background check for my new job. On Thursday, I received the information for my corporate training. The training would take place at the corporate headquarters in Virginia. The company paid for my flight and lodging; all other expenses would be reimbursed. My next focus was finding a place for Malachi while I was in Virginia.

I mentioned the trip to Royce, and he found a room for Malachi at a friend's house. Cousin Royce said he would take Malachi to school, pick him up, and feed him before dropping him off at the friend's house. I was nervous because I did not know the couple, but I trusted Royce. If he said they were good people, I believed him. Besides, I didn't really have another option. However, I did ask Royce to introduce me to the couple before I left.

The couple seemed nice enough, and I was glad Malachi would be taken care of when I went to Virginia. Unfortunately, we had to check out of the Intown Suites a few days before I was to leave, and again we needed somewhere to stay. I did not have the money for another week, so I had to trust that God would provide as He'd done before.

The day before our check-out date, I received a client's payment for a video I put together while we were at the Intown Suites. Miraculously, we also received funds from my Aunt Linda, and while I was thankful for the funds, it was not enough for us to stay at the Intown Suites or anywhere else.

Royce picked us up from the lobby on October 25th. I was anxious and prayerful because I had no clue where he would take us. I knew he didn't have enough room for us to stay at the Intown Suites again and frankly neither did I. I was out of options, but I had experienced God showing up in the nick of time before. I just had to trust He would do it again.

By the time Royce came to pick us up, I had communicated with my friend, Kindra. I told her we were checking out of the Intown Suites, and I was unsure what we would do next. We agreed that God would provide for Malachi and me again. When Royce arrived, we packed up his truck, and he asked me where we were going. I told him I was not sure but to head towards Bloomington.

We were on our way to Bloomington when Kindra called and told me the Lord had instructed her to give me $200. She had talked to her husband, Ron, and he agreed that they would help us. I could not believe it. Kindra and I rejoiced over the phone because God did it again, and we knew that if God told her to provide for me, then He would provide for her.

When I hung up with Kindra, Royce asked me about the call, and I told him that God provided, and he could take us to the Super 8 because we had enough. Kindra's donation secured us a three-night stay at the Super 8. That wasn't enough to last us until I left for Virginia, but it gave me three more days I didn't have to worry about. Grateful doesn't seem strong enough to describe the relief and thankfulness I felt.

When we arrived at Super 8, I got us a room. Royce helped us up with our things and told me he'd be in touch.

| 19 |

Taking Flight Again

We checked into the Super 8 and walked to get food. Unlike our previous stay, we could not get a room with a microwave and a refrigerator, but there was a microwave in the lobby that we could use to reheat food. We either had to make creative food choices or eat out, which we were both growing weary of doing.

Once we settled in our room, I strategized what time we needed to leave the next morning to get Malachi to school. It would be super early again, but I was confident we could get him there on time.

The next day, I decided to head back to the room after dropping Malachi off. For the next few days, I spent a lot of time in the room in prayer. I was thankful that I would start work soon and was grateful for an opportunity to provide for my family again.

The funds that Kindra and Ron sent were enough to get us three nights at the Super 8, but since I was leaving for training on the 30th, we would need two more nights before I left. I had learned early in the process that hotel points were valuable and could be used to get us low-cost or no-cost rooms. I had signed up for Wyndham Rewards years before our move to Minnesota but had no reason to use my points until now.

The night before we were to check out of the Super 8, I tried using my points online to get us another night, but for some reason, the system would not allow me, so I called their customer service line. I told the representative that I was trying to use a combination of points and cash to get a room for a night. After I told him what I was attempting to do, he said he would give me 200 extra points because I did not have enough points to complete the transaction. I'm not sure if he was supposed to do that, and I certainly did not ask him to do it, but I was thankful that he did. I was pretty sure it was a God thing.

When I hung up with customer service, I went to the front desk and extended our stay one more night. I needed another night to make it until I flew to Virginia, so I prayed and asked God to provide again.

The next day I received a message from a friend who wanted to know how she could send me money. She had been praying for us on our journey, but we hadn't talked in a while. She ended up sending the money via MoneyGram, so Malachi and I walked to the nearest location to receive it. We talked about many things while we walked to the MoneyGram, and I enjoyed hearing his point-of-view. Our walk together reminded me of the beauty that had come out of our challenging journey. Sharing one hotel room for so long had forced us to communicate and compromise. We had become not just family members but friends and allies.

When we arrived at the MoneyGram location, I realized it was a check-cashing place, and I hoped that my out-of-state license was enough for me to get the money. Thankfully it was. I had to sign a few different forms, but I walked out with the money my friend sent to us.

When I talked to her, I let her know the money was right on time. It was just enough to get us another night at the hotel. We arrived back at the hotel, and I finally booked our last night at the Super 8. I slept easy that night.

The next day Royce picked us up from the Super 8 and dropped me off at church. Since he would be taking care of Malachi for the week, Malachi went with him, and someone from church took me to the airport after service.

~~~

I boarded my flight to Virginia, thankful for the respite of hotel hopping and thankful that almost everything was taken care of for this training. During my communications about the trip, I got the impression that I would be able to take a hotel shuttle from the airport to the hotel. But when I arrived in Virginia and called the hotel, they told me they did not come to the airport, and I would need to take a cab. I was furious because the company said they would provide all transportation, so I had not made any other arrangements. I called the person in charge of logistics, and because it was Sunday, her line went to voicemail. I had no idea what I was going to do. After booking our last night at the Super 8, I only had a few dollars left, and I had planned to use that for dinner. I was frustrated, tired, and overwhelmed. This trip was my first time in this part of Virginia, and I was unprepared for this hiccup. I called my prayer partner because I needed help, and for the first time since taking my leap of faith, I asked for help. I hadn't come this far to get stuck at an airport.

My prayer partner agreed to help me, with cab fare from the airport. She suggested that I should try to share an Uber with someone else to save money. I had no idea you could even do that, but she told me how to pick that option in that app, and I was able to get to the hotel for a lot less than I thought.

The challenges continued when I got to the hotel. I walked up to the receptionist and was surprised to find out I had to use a credit card to check-in. It's funny that as many hotels as I'd stayed in, I'd assumed I wouldn't need to use my card for incidentals. Thankfully, they only held $25 for incidentals, and I actually had that on my card.

I took my bags to my room and decided to get some rest. I had to be up early so that I could take the shuttle to my new job for training. We ate a large meal at church before I left for the airport including fried chicken, macaroni and cheese, and so much more. It was delicious. Before leaving for the airport, several people at church insisted that I take some of the chicken with me for the road. By the time I arrived in my room, I was thankful for the blessing of fried chicken because it was too late to try to find food outside the hotel. I ate the chicken and a pastry

I picked up at the airport, took a shower, and climbed into bed. I was anxious to begin my new job and hopeful for the new start it would finally help us get in Minnesota.

I woke up ready to learn and eager for my first day at work. I got dressed, did my hair, and went to the lobby for breakfast. On my way to breakfast, I asked the receptionist about the shuttle to and she told me when it would leave.

At breakfast, I met quite a few of my new co-workers. Since our orientation fell on Halloween, costumes were welcomed if we decided to wear them. I should have guessed then that the company catered to a younger generation, but I needed a job, and I was excited about the opportunity.

| 20 |

Finding Home

During my first week of training for my new job, I trained during the day and at night, I looked for a place for us to live. Before I left for my training in Virginia, I decided to check local church announcements for possible apartment listings. Surprisingly, I found a beautiful lake house for rent.

The house looked amazing, and it was completely furnished, but I thought it had to be out of my price range. I decided to contact the owner, anyway. At this point, I had nothing to lose and possibly a beautiful rental home to gain. I called the number on the listing and left a message. While I was still in Virginia, the rental contact called me back and told me the house was available. The owner was out of the state, but she would be back over the weekend, and we could see it then. The woman on the phone said that if I liked the place, I could move right in. I asked her how much she wanted for the house, and she said, "You tell me."

For a minute, I was speechless. When I finally found my voice, I pitched a lease amount of $1,000 per month. The owner said she could work with that and promised to call to show us the house that weekend.

I had a few more days remaining of training in Virginia, but I had a new pep in my step because I thought for sure the lakehouse was the place for us. The ad said that the house was available from November until May, and at that point, that was good enough. When my training was complete, I flew back from Minnesota eager to see Malachi and tell him that we might have a new home on the lake. I was excited to see the place and hoped that it would be just what we needed.

When I arrived back in Minnesota, I called my cousin Royce to bring Malachi to me. Before I left, Royce told me that he would pay for us to get a room at the Super 8 once I got back. So, I took the airport shuttle to Super 8 and waited for Royce and Malachi in the lobby, but when they arrived, Royce told me that he found a better deal on a room somewhere else. He asked if we would be OK with that, and I told him that I was fine, as long as I could get a bus to work. He said he could get us three nights there, and then we'd be on our own.

The hotel was further out than I anticipated, but I accepted the room because we didn't have another choice. I had an appointment the next day to see the lake house, and I hoped that by the time Royce's three days were up, we'd be in our new lakefront home.

I made arrangements with my friend Calver to pick us up Saturday and take us to see the house. I was going to ask Jackie, but the Lord was clear that it needed to be Calver, so I asked her. She agreed, and I was thankful because there was no bus to the house on the weekends. I was ready to be in our place but super nervous. Calver prayed all the way there, and so did I.

When we arrived at the house, we could see the lake as we pulled up, and I was amazed. The owner was outside waiting for us, so I introduced myself and those who were with me. She walked us down the stairway to the house, and I was fascinated to see it was literally feet from the lake. I did not know which lake we were standing in front of, but it was beautiful.

When she opened the door to the house, I could see that it was a split level. As we entered the front door, we could either go upstairs to the main living level or downstairs to the basement. We went to the main living level first, and it was breathtaking. Off to the right was the living room with a large picture window that faced the lake.

Across from the living room was the well-appointed kitchen and fully furnished dining room. The dining room had beautiful French doors that looked out onto the lake, so you could enjoy the view while having meals.

On the other side of the stairs, there were two bedrooms and a large bathroom. The bedrooms had more beds in them than we needed. The master bedroom had two full-size beds, and the second bedroom had two sets of bunk beds. When we went downstairs, there was another partially finished bedroom. The walls needed to be completed, but it was still a viable room, complete with a bed and linens. Malachi chose that room for himself. There was also a 3/4 bathroom in the basement, along with a laundry room and a game room. She even had a Christmas tree we could use when it came time to put up decorations.

I was so thankful and happy. I couldn't believe all of this could be ours. It was a beautiful home, and I felt such peace there. I found out later that the owner held prayer meetings in the house, and I knew that's why I felt that peace. I was in complete awe of how wonderfully God had provided. I was determined to tell the whole world of His goodness.

The house was perfect for us, and I was excited about it. The owner told me that if I had the money, we could move in that day. I told her I did not have the money right then, but I would have it soon. I was honestly speaking in faith because I needed $2000 to move in. I did not have that, and my first paycheck was probably not going to be that much, but I trusted that God would provide. She told me to call her when I was ready.

I was anxious to have a home again and grateful that this house came with everything we needed. The homeowner even provided dish detergent. We could literally just unpack and start living. I just knew God had set this house aside for us. I recorded the entire house tour because I knew that we were going to move in. When I stood out on the porch taking the video, I began to weep in awe of God's faithfulness. He had thought of every detail. I always knew that I needed to live near the water because it jolts my creativity. On all accounts, the lakehouse was perfect.

We finished the tour, and Calver drove us back to the hotel. She asked me if I had the money, and I told her that I didn't, but I believed God. She said she did too. We prayed in faith that God would do it, and the peace of God covered me in the car. I didn't know how, but I was sure God would provide what we needed to secure our home. When Calver dropped us off at the hotel, she told me that she would pick us up for church in the morning but that someone else would need to bring us back. I was thankful because I really needed to get to church.

The next day we went to church, and another couple, Mel and Cherie, volunteered to take us back to the hotel since it was close to their house. When we got ready to leave, I asked Cherie if she would take us to a store on the way to the hotel so I could get a few toiletries. Cherie said we would go to her house first, and then we could go to the store from there. I was a little confused, but I just said OK.

When we got to her house, she told me that she and her husband wanted to let me drive their vehicle for a couple of hours so I could get what I needed without feeling rushed. She told me they would just come to the hotel later that evening to pick it up from me. She also handed me a $20 bill that someone had given her for me. I was surprised they let me use their car and thankful for the donated funds.

We left Cherie's house, and I searched my GPS for a store close to the hotel. We ended up at the Cub Foods – a local grocery chain - near the hotel and because we had the vehicle, I was able to take my time and get what we needed. We decided that since we were leaving the hotel the next morning, we would eat out and not buy a bunch of food.

When we left Cub, we stopped by a fast-food restaurant where I had coupons and picked up dinner. We headed back to the hotel, parked the car, and headed into the room. Once we ate, I gathered our clothes and washed them in the hotel's laundry room because I wanted us to be ready for the next day.

While I waited for our laundry, I decided to call my Aunt Kneata because I needed to check in with her. I knew she was worried about us, and I wanted to put her mind at ease by telling her things were beginning to work out. I told her that I was working and had a prospect for a place. I let her know that we only had to stay in a hotel for a few more days, and I believed God would provide a room since I did not get paid for a few more days.

She was happy that I was working, and she told me that she would see if she could arrange some things to help us out. She promised to get back to me and let me know. By the time I headed to bed, I had enough money from Aunt Kneata and other family members to book us a room at the Super 8 for a few more days. I had no idea where we would go after the funds were exhausted, but I knew that God had not brought us this far to leave us. Things were finally turning around, and I knew that it was just a matter of time before everything panned out completely.

The next day, I made sure everything was packed and ready to go so Malachi and Royce could just grab our things and leave. I had to be at work by 8:30 am, and the checkout time was at 11 am, so my cousin Royce agreed to come to the hotel to get Malachi after I left. Royce checked us out of the hotel, loaded our things into his truck, and took Malachi to school for me. He also picked Malachi up from school and brought him to the Super 8, where we would stay for the next few days.

I checked us into the Super 8, and once we got our bags in the room, I ordered food from Papa John's and tried to figure out how I would get Malachi to school and myself to work the next morning. He had to be at school before 7:30 am, and I had to be to work by 8:30 am but getting all of that done was a challenge without a car. However, I figured out that if we left super early, we could catch the bus, and both of us could reach our destinations on time.

The next day, we left early like we were supposed to, but we got off the bus at the wrong stop. The first bus we took was not a bus we'd taken before, so I was a bit disoriented when we exited. Unfortunately, it didn't dawn on me to ask the driver where we needed to go to get the next bus.

We got off the first bus and walked up to the bus stop on the highway, not realizing we were on the wrong side of the road. Soon, we saw our bus pass by on the opposite side. I thought maybe we could catch the next one, but we missed it too. There was no way for Malachi to get to school on time, so reluctantly, I took Malachi back to the hotel, and I went on to work. On our way to yet another bus stop, he tripped and fell, and I knew we had both hit our limit. My son was tired, and frankly, so was I; I just wanted this madness of moving every few days to be over.

We finally got on the bus back to the hotel and sat in the front of the bus. I dropped Malachi off at the hotel and let him head up to the room while I continued onto my job. Despite the craziness of the morning, I still made it work on time, but I was exhausted and ready for a nap. I was thankful that the office had free coffee, but I wished I could get espresso shots because I was still in training and needed to focus. Unfortunately, several cups of coffee and water had to suffice.

While I was in one of my training sessions, I received a call from the housing division of Hennepin County. They told me the lakehouse owner had made arrangements to allow Malachi and me to move into the house without any out-of-pocket cost for me. The housing department paid the security and the first month's rent for the home, so all I needed to do was meet up with the owners, sign the lease and move in.

As soon as I hung up with the housing department, I received a call from the homeowner, and she told me that we could move in that day since the housing group promised to send a check, and she was confident she would get it. I was so happy and thankful that it was hard to compose myself and get back to work. No one at my job knew I was basically homeless. Malachi and I were not on the streets, but neither did we have a steady place to go to. I sent Jackie a text and told her that we were able to move into the lakehouse that night, and she agreed to pick us up when I got off work and take us out to our new home.

I felt like I was working in slow motion the rest of the day. Time seemed to creep by. During my break, I contacted Malachi's counselor to let her know that we were finally moving into our home and asked her if they could expedite our transportation request. She let me know that our new location would be added to the bus route in a few days. I was relieved that I no longer had to worry about getting my son back and forth to school.

When my workday was finally over, I headed back to the hotel to pack up and tell Malachi the fantastic news. We were both relieved and happy to finally have a home, and not just any home, a beautiful lake house.

Jackie arrived not long after I did, and we packed up her car and checked out of the hotel. We got to the house, and Jackie helped us with our things. I was glad that she was the one to help us cross the threshold on our first day living in the lake house. Jackie had been an essential part of our journey in Minnesota. She helped us from the beginning to the end, and I felt blessed to share move-in day with her.

It was the first time Jackie saw the house and only the second time that I'd seen it, and it was stunningly beautiful. The owner presented me with the lease, and I signed it. We were finally in a home of our own – a home with a bedroom for each of us and a kitchen for serving homecooked meals. I was overwhelmed and grateful.

After our first tour of the home, I had started looking into transportation because I knew I would not have a car right away. The lakehouse was on the outskirts of town, so I knew I would need a dependable way to get to work and back home. I also needed to figure out how to get Malachi to school until the bus started picking him up.

It took us a few weeks to get acquainted with our new home. After doing a little research, I found out that the same Southwest Prime bus that Malachi often caught when we were in hotels, serviced the area where we now lived. My trip, however, was a little more complicated. I had to take the Southwest Prime bus from the lake house to an express bus station, then take an express bus to a city bus that would drop me off at work. My commute started at 6 am and ended when I arrived at the office at 8:30 am. It was grueling and, at times, frustrating, but I was willing to do whatever I needed to do to stay in this house.

The first few days after moving into the lake house, I had trouble finding out the correct timing, and consequentially, missed a few days of work. But I kept pushing forward, and soon, I had the commute to work down to a science. Getting back home was another matter altogether. My day ended at 5 pm, but I had to take a city bus to an express station in downtown Minneapolis and then hope the express bus would transport me in time to catch the Southwest Prime, which ran from 6 am – 6 pm. The first few weeks, I struggled getting home, but I was determined to figure it out. I believed God had a plan for me, and I would not allow frustrations to get in the way. Instead of Southwest Prime, I started using Lyft to get home. I also figured out that Metro Transit would pick me up at the office and bring me home directly if I called ahead of time to schedule a ride. My days were excruciatingly long, but I was adjusting.

Each time I looked out at the lake – day or night – I was thankful. Each time I was able to make a home-cooked meal, I was thankful. I was grateful to be settled in our place, finally. All of the moving from place to place - the uncertainty, fears, frustrations, doubts, and insecurities had been for a purpose. When I signed the lease for the lake house, I understood that there is nothing impossible for God. I was humbled by the sheer magnitude of what God did for us, and I wanted to share it with the world.

While we only had six months at the Lake House, I was determined to be thankful for the moment and, I refused to worry about what the future held. I knew my faith journey was just beginning, but I took the opportunity to rest in the serenity of the lake house.

What I realized is that while the lake house was beautiful there was a deeper revelation for me. God wanted to show me that He was my source and that I could count on Him to provide. No, he was not going to drop money from heaven, but He used people to help us.

As we settled into the lake house, I started a new prayer assignment – a prayer ministry here in the Twin Cities. It was something that I was unsure about because I did not think I was qualified enough, but after our journey of faith, I knew that I could do it.

Not long after I launched the prayer ministry, I was praying for people all over the Twin Cities and it all began to make sense – the struggle, the tears, the prayers, the journey, and the increase in my faith – it was all necessary to get to this point of ministry and I was thankful for every part of it. My faith allowed me to pray for people who needed to be empowered, transformed, and set free. I was thankful to God for the ability to pray for others. I was thankful for the journey and thankful that God allowed me to be used this way. For me, it was just the beginning.

| 21 |

Losing Yet Gaining Everything

Now that you've read my story and followed me through the painful details that threatened to suffocate me in the middle of my faith walk, let's talk about how it feels to lose everything. As I looked at the empty place where my 2008 Ford Edge was supposed to be parked, my heart hurt, but my faith in God was sure. When I was evicted from our home of three years, I was ashamed, but I committed to trusting God. When I had to take my son from his friends and family, I was devastated, but I chose obedience.

Being faithful is at odds with our natural inclinations. Submitting to God's process must be deliberate, and it will not be comfortable. I'm sure everyone who knew me thought I was crazy when I walked away from a steady paycheck to invest in my businesses. The whispers grew even louder when I took my son and moved to an unknown city. I knew there were whispers and looks. There were conversations about the effect my choices were having on Malachi. But the talk didn't matter because I knew God had called me, and I knew I would be held responsible for what I did next.

I understood the confusion, though. Up until my leap, I also had a limited concept of faith. But all of that changed because God showed me just how omnipotent He is. I have been forever changed. I was passionate enough to seek God and radically obey Him. That obedience cost me dearly, and yet, I still had everything I needed. God provided for me just like I thought He would. I may have felt like I was losing my mind, but one thing I knew was I was never alone.

I realize now that trying to keep God in the box of my comfort and understanding only limits His room to be God in my life. If I am going to trust Him to deliver, provide, save, and forgive, then I have to give Him the space to move. Were there times of doubt and uncertainty? Absolutely! You can't go out into the water this deep without questioning your sanity, but I knew that as long as I kept my eyes on God, we'd be fine.

On this side of some of the storms, I realize that we're more than fine. We've grown and evolved. We're stronger, less influenced by the whims of man, and more focused on God's voice. Our faith has been tested, and it has come out in a much purer form. The faith I have now is to believe God for the impossible and trust Him with my life. My faith has empowered me, transformed me, and set me free.

I appreciate you going on this journey with me, but now let me ask you, what are you waiting for? What has God asked of you, and when are you going to leap?

THE END

FOOTNOTES

1. ^ 2 Corinthians 12:9
2. ^ Philippians 4:6

ABOUT THE AUTHOR

Liela Marie Fuller is the author of six books, including Life's Reflection and Love Letters of a Worshipper. She is also the creator of six journals, including Don't Stop Knocking, Don't Stop Seeking, Don't Stop Praying, and Don't Stop Believing: A Prayer Journal. Liela is originally from Camden, NJ, but currently resides in Minnesota. You can connect with Liela on Facebook, Twitter, Instagram, and on her website – www.ThoughtsofaThankfulHeart.com.

www.ingramcontent.com/pod-product-compliance
Lightning Source LLC
Chambersburg PA
CBHW050438010526
44118CB00013B/1584